Building Citizenship: Civics and Economics

READING ESSENTIALS & STUDY GUIDE

Answer Key

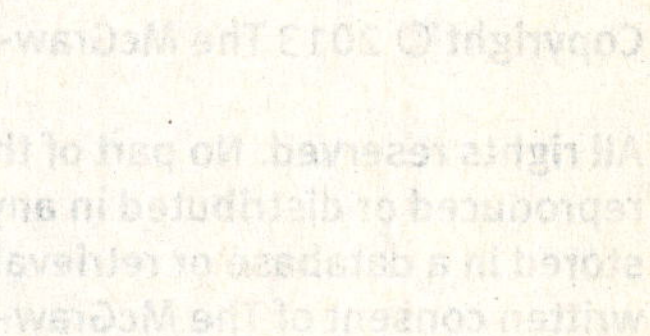

Bothell, WA • Chicago, IL • Columbus, OH • New York, NY

Cover Photo Credit:
Romy Vandenberg/Wesend61/Corbis

connected.mcgraw-hill.com

Send all inquiries to:
McGraw-Hill Education
8787 Orion Place
Columbus, OH 43240

ISBN: 978-0-07-660013-7
MHID: 0-07-660013-0

Printed in the United States of America.

9 10 11 12 13 14 QVS 20 19 18 17 16

The McGraw·Hill Companies

Table of Contents

The Judicial Branch

Political Parties

Voting and Elections

Public Opinion and Government

State Government

Local Government

Dealing with Community Issues

Citizens and the Law

Civil and Criminal Law

networks

Notebook Foldables®

Using Foldables® in the *Reading Essentials and Study Guide* will help your students develop note-taking and critical-thinking skills while directly interacting with the text.

Templates allow students to make their own Notebook Foldables®.

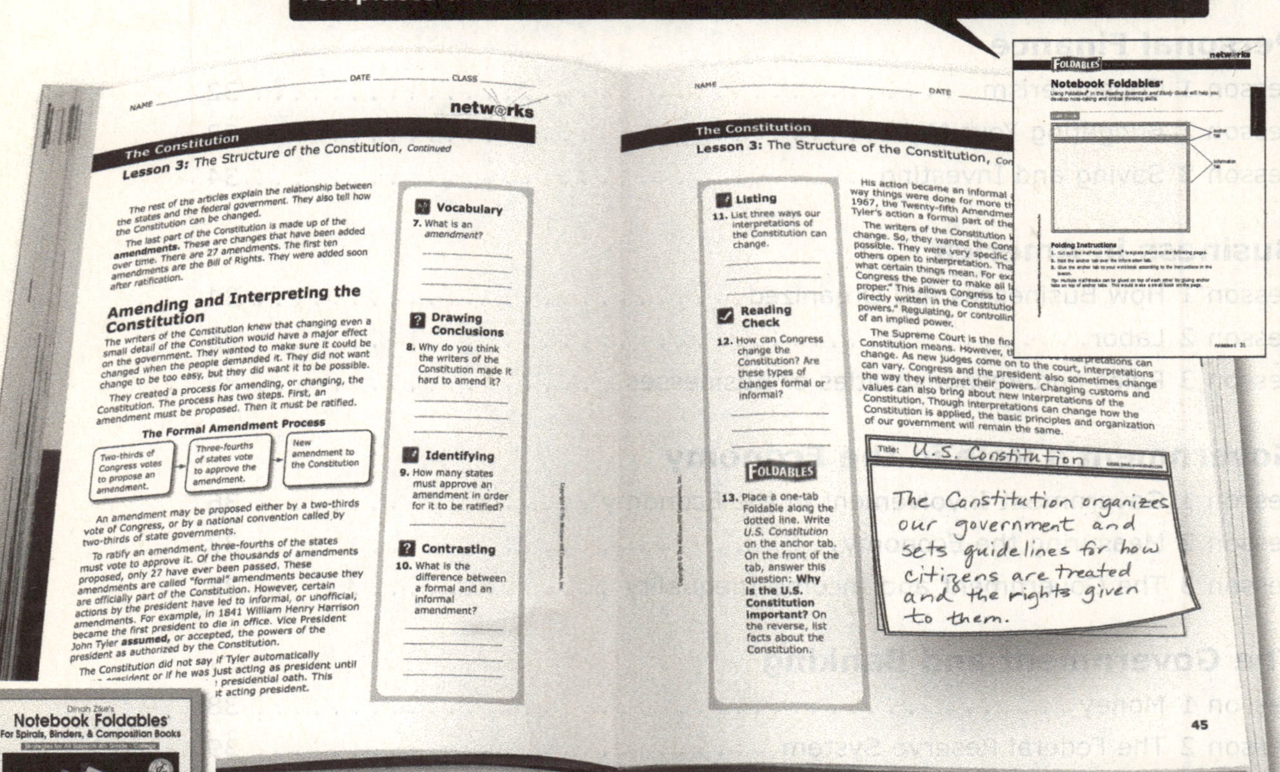

The *Reading Essentials and Study Guide* extends learning with Dinah Zike's award winning Notebook Foldables®. Notebook Foldables are specially designed to fit in workbooks and composition books. In partnership with Dinah, McGraw-Hill has developed the *Reading Essentials and Study Guide* with Notebook Foldables® to engage students more fully in social studies content.

It is easy to make Notebook Foldables®

1. **FOLD** an anchor tab and the desired number of information tabs.
2. **GLUE** the anchor tab.
3. **CUT** information tabs.

Students will master social studies concepts, ideas, and facts as they complete the side margin activities in this workbook, along with the many Notebook Foldables activities placed within the pages.

To the Teacher

Dear Teacher,

Considerable research indicates that students need to know how to take notes, use graphic organizers, and develop their critical-thinking skills through writing in order to achieve academic success. For the struggling student, this can be an overwhelming task. McGraw-Hill has developed this workbook to help such students clarify content and make connections. This *Reading Essentials and Study Guide* will help students master content and develop skills necessary for academic success.

This workbook includes all core content found in the *Building Citizenship: Civics and Economics* program. The simplified manner and tools of the workbook help the approaching-level reader grasp the content and concepts. The note-taking, graphic organizer, and Foldables activities enable students to unpack and organize content for improved comprehension and testing.

Note-Taking System

You will notice that the pages in the *Reading Essentials and Study Guide* are arranged in two columns, which is based on the Cornell Note-Taking system developed at Cornell University. The large column on the page contains running text and graphics that summarize each lesson of the chapter. These summaries are written at a lower level to help struggling readers comprehend the content. The smaller column helps students find and use information in various ways and focus on the important information of the lesson. Students will use recognized reading strategies to improve comprehension. As students become more comfortable using the Cornell Note-Taking System, they will see that it helps them organize their thoughts as well as the information.

Graphic Organizers

Many graphic organizers appear in this workbook. Graphic organizers allow students to see the lesson's important information in a visual format. In addition, graphic organizers help students summarize information and remember the content. The *Reading Essentials and Study Guide* includes maps, flowcharts, graphs, and tables that are designed with student learning in mind.

Notebook FOLDABLES®

Notebook Foldables®, invented by Dinah Zike, M.Ed., show students how to make interactive graphic organizers based upon skills. Foldables are easy to create and quickly engage the student in the content. Every Notebook Foldable® is placed directly within the content pages, extending learning and note-taking capabilities. Making a Foldable® gives students a fast, kinesthetic activity that helps them organize and retain information. Each Notebook Foldable® is designed as a study guide for the main ideas and key points presented in lessons of the chapter. Notebook Foldables® help unpack difficult concepts, ideas, and terms studied in a lesson.

The *Reading Essentials and Study Guide* is a thoroughly interactive student workbook that will immerse students in social studies content. Students will master the content while learning important critical-thinking and note-taking skills that they will use throughout their lives.

FOLDABLES®

Notebook Foldable® Basics

Notebook Foldables® are an easy, unique way to enhance learning. Instructions are located at point of use and every template is provided at the back of the student workbook. Students cut out the appropriate Foldable® template and place it into the workbook as instructed. This quickly turns a workbook into a hands-on learning and study guide.

Using Notebook Foldables®

Students will write information such as titles, vocabulary words, concepts, questions, main ideas, summaries, definitions, and dates on the tabs of their Foldables®. This will help students easily recognize main ideas and important concepts as they review content.

In the back of the student workbook are several pages with four different Foldable® style templates – one-tab, two-tab, three-tab, and Venn diagram. Each style has an instruction page followed by the templates. Cutting and using the different templates is very simple to master.

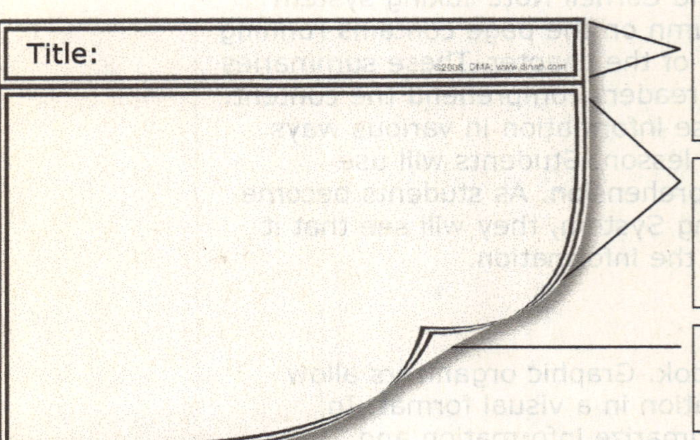

Anchor Tab– Glue the back of the Foldable to the workbook with the anchor tab. A dotted line is provided on the workbook page to guide Students to proper placement.

Information Tab – Write information on the front and reverse of the information tab. This tab may be cut again after gluing if it is a two-, three-, or Venn diagram style.

Reverse Information Tab

Folding Instructions

1. **Cut** out the appropriate Foldable® template.
2. **Fold** the anchor tab over the information tab.
3. **Glue** the anchor tab to the workbook page according to the instructions. *(Just a dab is needed!)*

Multiple Foldables® can be glued on top of each other by gluing anchor tabs on top of anchor tabs. This would make a small book on the page.

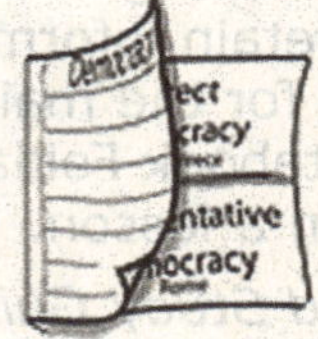

Supplies

The only supplies needed to utilize Notebook Foldables® are scissors and glue. All paper templates are in the back of the workbook. If it is difficult for your students to provide glue and scissors, set up a small space in the classroom with several pairs of scissors and small containers of glue. Consider supplying containers of crayons and colored pencils, a stapler, clear tape, and anything else you think students might like to make their Foldables® more interesting. Such creative opportunities can enrich the learning moment and make a lasting impression of the content.

Who is Dinah Zike?

Dinah Zike, M.Ed., is an award-winning author, educator, and inventor known for designing three-dimensional hands-on manipulatives and graphic organizers known as Foldables®. Foldables® are used nationally and internationally by teachers, parents, and educational publishing companies. Dinah has developed more than 150 supplemental educational books and materials. Her two latest books, *Notebook Foldables®* and *Foldables®, Notebook Foldables®, & VKV®s for Spelling and Vocabulary 4th-12th* were each awarded *Learning* Magazine's Teachers' Choice Award for 2011. In 2004, Dinah was honored with the Council for Elementary Science International (CESI) Science Advocacy Award. Dinah received her M.Ed. from Texas A&M, College Station, Texas. Dinah has been a valued contributing editor to the McGraw-Hill K-12 education programs for many years.

Reading Essentials and Study Guide

Answer Key

Americans, Citizenship, and Governments, Lesson 1

What Do You Know?

Freedom, justice, and democracy

Lesson Activities

A Diverse Population

1. Almost all of the people in the United States come from families who once lived in another country.
2. Asia
3. 1970; 1890 and 1910
4. enslaved Africans
5. Beginning in the 1890s, more immigrants to the U.S. came from southern and eastern Europe rather than from northern and western Europe as they had previously.
6. The cities often promised jobs and a better life.
7. ethnic group
8. Hispanic, Native Hawaiian and other Pacific Islander
9. Hispanic

Values and Institutions

10. answers will vary
11. The family is the center of social life and teaches children values.
12. the Declaration of Independence and the Constitution
13. family, religion, clubs and volunteer groups
14. *First Americans:* Native Americans were the first people to live in America. They immigrated to America from Asia thousands of years before other immigrants. *Other Immigrants:* came to America in the 1500's from countries around the world to make it their home; *Forming America*: Over hundreds of years, government and institutions were created in America based upon shared values.

Check for Understanding

1-2. Native Americans were the first to settle in North America. They came from Asia.

3. Our government institutions were set up to protect our freedom to live without arbitrary meddling from the government, and they are based on the idea of popular sovereignty. In addition, the Constitution limits the power of government by dividing it into three parts. No one part can have more power than the others.

Americans, Citizenship, and Governments, Lesson 2

What Do You Know?

It means someone is loyal to a government and is protected by that government.

A person who lives in a country in which he or she was not born and stay in the country illegally. They do not have the rights of citizens or those who stay in the country legally.

Lesson Activities

What Is Civics?

1. to understand our rights and responsibilities as citizens
2. students should draw a timeline titled "The Growth of American Citizenship," with the events in the following order: **1776** White men who owned property **1868** African American men win citizenship through the 14th Amendment **1920** Women win the right to vote through the 19th Amendment **1924** All Native Americans are granted citizenship
3. Students should circle "the 14th Amendment" and "the 19th Amendment."
4. Students should circle the phrase "based on birth."
5. yes, they are a natural-born citizen
6. A person must be at least 18 years old, have been a legal permanent resident for five years, be able to read, write, and speak English, be of good moral character, and show that they understand U.S. civics.
7. the U.S. Citizenship and Immigration Service
8. An oath is a promise or swearing to something. It is part of the last step of naturalization, the citizenship ceremony.

9. **Expatriation**: If a person gives allegiance to another country, such as by becoming a naturalized citizen of another country. **Denaturalization**: If a person is found to have lied on his or her citizenship application, he or she loses citizenship and can be deported. To be deported is to be sent out of the country. **Being convicted of certain crimes**: If a person is convicted of treason, rebelling against the government, or using violence to try to overthrow the government he or she can lose citizenship.

Foreign-Born Residents

10. A resident alien lives permanently in the U.S., while a nonresident alien lives in the U.S. for only a certain length of time.
11. While legal aliens have some rights, such as attending public schools and owning property, they cannot vote, hold public office, work in the government, or serve on juries.
12. *Citizen by birth*: A person born in the United States or who has parents born in the United States. *Citizen by Naturalization*: Immigrants can become naturalized citizens by meeting five requirements: 18 years old; legal permanent resident for five years; read, write, speak English; good moral character; and demonstrate an understanding of U.S. civics. *Aliens*: Many people who live in the U.S. are not citizens. There are three groups of aliens: legal, illegal, and refugees.

Check for Understanding

1-2. legal permanent resident for five years; able to read, write, and speak English; of good moral character; understand U.S. civics

3. They come seeking a better life.

Americans, Citizenship, and Governments, Lesson 3

What Do You Know?

taxes keep the government running

respecting and accepting others

volunteering meets the needs of many who cannot fulfill those needs themselves

Lesson Activities

Duties of Citizens

1. responsibilities: things we should do. Duties: things we have to do.
2. to keep order in society
3. government: pay its employees, defend the country, help those in need. state: run schools, pave roads, hire firefighters
4. The government would have to draft male citizens.

Responsibilities of Citizens

5. It is required by law.
6. because government decisions affect your life
7. It gives citizens a voice in government and is a peaceful way to transfer power.
8. Because the population in this country is so diverse, people may have very different opinions on important issues. Tolerance is necessary to keep society functioning.
9. the practice of offering your time and service to others without receiving payment
10. Students should underline the sentence that reads "More than one million charities are registered with the federal government."
11. Americorps
12. *Responsibilities*: those things we should do; things we do as citizens of our own free will for the betterment of the community. *Duties*: things we are required to do by law.

Check for Understanding

1-2. obey the law; pay taxes; defend the nation if drafted, serve in court, attend school

3-4. Possible answers include be informed and vote, participate in government and your community, respect the rights and property of others, respect different opinions and ways of life.

5. volunteering time or donating money to help others

Americans, Citizenship, and Governments, Lesson 4

What Do You Know?

Governments make and carry out laws and decisions for those living in a community.

representative democracy

Lesson Activities

The Importance of Government

1. by establishing and enforcing laws
2. services to protect public health, public safety, and public welfare
3. Possible answers: the president, senators, representatives, mayor, governor, town council

4. power is divided between the national government and the states
5. State governments make laws and public policies only for the people within the state, while the federal government makes laws and policies for the entire nation.
6. Local government helps the local community by setting up police and fire departments and local courts. They also provide services like lighting the streets and removing snow.

The Types of Government

7. *Representative Majority* allows citizens to play a part in selecting the head of the government. *Constitutional Monarchy* has a ceremonial head of government that inherits the position. *Both*: governing officials are elected, the majority rules, the minority maintains rights
8. Democracy uses majority rule, which means that citizens agree that they will abide by what most people want.
9. democracy: the people rule, the people have freedoms, the people can criticize the government. authoritarian regimes: one person or a small group holds all the power, the people do not have freedoms, the people cannot criticize the government
10. absolute monarch and dictatorship
11. In an absolute monarchy, all power rests with the monarch. Constitutional monarchies are democratic (power lies with the people). Monarchs have mostly ceremonial and social duties.
12. A federal system of government shares power between a central government and smaller units of government, such as states. In a unitary system, all power rests with the central government.
13. *Purpose*: Governments make and carry out laws so people can live together peacefully, resolve conflicts, provide national security, and provide other public services to protect public health, safety, and welfare. *Types*: Nations have many forms of government including those where the people rule (democracies) and those where one person or group rules (authoritarian regimes). There are two types of representational democracy—republics and constitutional monarchies. The United States is a republic.

Check for Understanding

1. Government allows people to live together in peace, rather than in fear and violence.
2. In a direct democracy, every eligible citizen takes part in discussing and voting on issues. Today's nations are too large for direct democracy to be practical.

The American Colonies and Their Government, Lesson 1

What Do You Know?

People need government to help organize society and make peaceful living easier.

Lesson Activities

The Foundations of Democracy

1. Democracy is a government in which the people rule.
2. Democracy is a government ruled by the people. Greece gave us the first direct democracy which allows all the citizens to take part in government and govern themselves. Rome gave us representative democracy which chooses a group of leaders to govern the citizens.
3. The Magna Carta gave landowners the right to trial by their peers and the right to equal treatment under the law.
4. It prohibited the king from doing certain things.
5. It was the official paper that Parliament made King John sign; it introduced the idea of limited government.
6. The change in government that happened when Parliament forced King James II from power and asked Mary and her husband William to rule instead.

Influence of the Enlightenment

7. Students should circle, "The problems between the monarchy and Parliament created new ideas about government. These ideas were part of a movement in Europe known as the Enlightenment."
8. the right to life, the right to freedom, and the right to own property
9. Students should circle, "Locke said that people form governments to protect their natural rights. Natural rights are rights that everyone should have. These include the right to life, the right to freedom, and the right to own property." Students should underline, "According to the social contract, the people agreed to give up some freedom and be ruled by government. In return, the government agreed to protect the people's rights. If it did not do that, the contract was broken. If the contract was broken, then the people could choose new leaders."
10. an agreement

The First Colonial Governments

11. Jamestown; Plymouth
12. direct democracy

13. a strong belief in democracy and representative government

14. Answers will vary but may include the Enlightenment, limited government, the Glorious Revolution, English Bill of Rights, natural rights, social contract, protecting citizen's rights, democracy, right to freedom, to own property, and life.

Check for Understanding

1-3. limited power of government, natural rights, democracy, social contract, English Bill of Rights.

The American Colonies and Their Government, Lesson 2

What Do You Know?

People came for land, to find jobs, and to escape religious persecution.

In New England, most people lived in towns. In the Middle and Southern Colonies, most people farmed and raised crops.

Lesson Activities

Settling the English Colonies

1. They were too poor to pay the cost of coming on their own, so they agreed to work off their debt to those who paid their passage.

2. religious freedom and economic opportunity

3. The founders of Rhode Island were dissenters. They disagreed with the religious beliefs of the Puritans.

Colonial Life

4. Both came for religious freedom, as well as land and a better life, their only difference was how they worshipped.

5. New England's farms were small as they were not as fertile as farms elsewhere, like the South.

6. the wheat trade, trade in other cash crops, and trade in natural resources

7. tobacco, indigo

8. The closer related industries were, the more inexpensive it is to create products. If there are many lumber industries near shipbuilding industries, it is easier and cheaper to make ships.

9. cold, cash, rich, cash crops

10. Southern colonies had many large farms called plantations, where as in New England the farms were usually small.

11. the plantation owners, because they were rich and powerful

Colonial Government

12. The colonists began to depend on their local leaders because messages took so long to get back and forth between England and the colonies.

13. The English government began by paying little attention to the colonies, but by the 1650s, Parliament was passing laws to regulate colonial trade.

14. *New England*: Massachusetts, New Hampshire, Connecticut, Rhode Island; people mostly lived in towns; soil was rock and the climate was cold; much shipbuilding and fishing; *Middle Colonies*: New York, Pennsylvania, New Jersey, Delaware; cash crop farming; crops shipped overseas, rich with lumber, metals and harbors; *Southern Colonies*: Maryland, Virginia, North Carolina, South Carolina, Georgia; large plantations, warm with rich soil, many enslaved people, few towns and cities

Check for Understanding

1-3. New England Colonies: cold climate, rocky soil, small farms, many people lived in towns; Middle Colonies: cash crops, good soil for wheat, rich in natural resources; Southern Colonies: plantations, warm climate, long growing season, plantation owners ran the government

4-5. They made laws, taxed the colonists, and decided how to use the tax revenue.

The American Colonies and Their Government, Lesson 3

What Do You Know?

The Great Awakening and the Enlightenment changed the colonists' ideas about Britain.

The colonists were angry about being taxed to pay for the French and Indian War and various taxes and other laws passed by the British government.

It was written to address grievances that the colonists had with the king that had been growing for some time.

Lesson Activities

Social and Political Changes in the Colonies

1. The power to make others obey; students should underline *traditional, to question*

2. *The Great Awakening:* 1740s; they began to challenge the authority of the church and political leaders, they wanted more liberty and rights

The French and Indian War: 1763; the war debt caused the king to place taxes and harsh rules on the colonists. They began to resent this and having a distant ruler.

3. No; the colonists did not get enough land because they were forbidden to move onto it.

4. to raise money to help pay for the French and Indian War

5. They wanted more land, and they thought Great Britain was trying to limit their growth.

Colonial Dissatisfaction Grows

6. Quartering Act

7. made colonists buy and place tax stamps on, tax, British officials

8. The Tea Act made British tea cheaper than American tea. Thus, people would tend to buy more British tea than other tea sold in the colonies. This would negatively affect colonial tea merchants.

9. They searched peoples homes to see if the import duty had been paid and were meant to stop smuggling.

10. because the laws were so harsh

Steps Toward Independence

11. boycott

12. Second Continental Congress; January 1776; Declaration of Independence approved

13. to talk about or argue; students should underline *delegates, met,* and *what to do*

14. Thomas Paine used some of John Locke's ideas to make his case.

15. Students should underline *Voltaire, Jean-Jacques Rousseau, John Locke*. Their ideas combined guided Jefferson's writing of the Declaration of Independence.

Check for Understanding

1-2. Any two: the Enlightenment, Common Sense, the Great Awakening

3-4. because of the Proclamation of 1783, the Coercive Acts, the other Acts

The Constitution, Lesson 1

What Do You Know?

State governments each had constitutions, legislatures, governors, and courts.

The Articles of Confederation limited the powers of Congress so that it could not collect taxes or enforce laws, making it weak and unable to help the independent nation.

Lesson Activities

State Constitutions

1. As independence neared, they needed plans for government to replace the colonial charters.

2. a detailed, written plan for government

The Articles of Confederation

3. They could not fight a war with 13 separate armies.

4. a group that comes together for a common purpose

5. Major waterways bring in goods from other places, people, and food. Waterways make travel much easier than roadways, meaning growth of townships is easier.

6. Answers will vary, but students should understand that colonists, having lived under British tyranny, were wary of governmental power.

7. The national and state governments were in debt, taxes were high, trade was slow, and people suffered.

8. There were strict voting rules: The legislature could not pass a law unless nine states voted for it.

9. the states

10. The Articles did not give Congress the powers it needed to fix these problems.

11. Delegates meet to strengthen the Articles of Confederation.

12. Constitution: a written plan of government; Bicameral legislature: a government divided into two parts; Governor: a leader to carry out the laws; Court system: decides how to apply the laws

Check for Understanding

1-2. They wrote state constitutions, organized legislatures, named governors, and developed a system of courts.

3-4. It was hard to pass laws because 9 of the 13 states had to agree; all 13 states had to agree before the articles could be changed; Congress had no power to collect taxes; Congress did not have the power to enforce laws.

The Constitution, Lesson 2

What Do You Know?

The Articles of Confederation were not strong enough and too flawed to be fixed.

Lesson Activities

The Constitutional Convention

1. Answers will vary.
2. so that they could discuss ideas and make decisions without anyone else interfering

Compromising for a Constitution

3. Many Americans felt that the Confederation government was too weak to deal with the nation's problems.
4. Virginia Plan
5. An agreement in which each side gives up something and gets something else.
6. *Virginia Plan*: The small states did not like it because it gave more power to the large states. Large states liked it because the number of delegates would be based on population so would give them more power in government. *New Jersey Plan*: Small states liked it because all would have equal votes regardless of size. Large states did not like it because this gave them no increased power. *Both* kinds of states liked the Great Compromise because it included equal seats in one house and seats based on population in another.
7. Each state gave up some control of Congress. Small states agreed to proportional representation in the House. Large states agreed to equal representation in the Senate.
8. Americans viewed enslaved people as property rather than as human beings entitled to all the rights promised in the Constitution.

Federalists and Anti-federalists

9. The Federalists supported ratifying the Constitution because they thought the system of federalism would solve the nation's problems.
10. It is a form of government in which power is divided between the federal and state governments.
11. Federalists believed the nation needed a strong central government to survive. Anti-federalists believed a strong central government would trample the rights of the state and the people.
12. Federalists: believed in a strong central government and that the new constitution would divide power between the national and state government; Anti-Federalists: believed a strong central government was not good and that the states should have the most power; Both: believed a bill of rights was needed

Check for Understanding

1-2. establishing the House of Representatives and the Senate; Congress given the power to make laws about trade; direct election of the president of the people; the Three-Fifths Compromise

The Constitution, Lesson 3

What Do You Know?

The Constitution organizes the government to keep it fair and its power balanced

yes; amendments to the Constitution can be made

Lesson Activities

The Parts of the Constitution

1. the Preamble
2. the Preamble, the Articles, and the Amendments
3. the Articles
4. Students should underline *They describe how the government is to be set up.*
5. the legislative, executive, and judicial branches
6. Congress makes laws. The executive branch carries out laws and enforces laws. The judicial branch makes sure that laws are applied fairly.
7. It is a change to the Constitution.

Amending and Interpreting the Constitution

8. Answers will vary, but should reflect that amendments are not to be undertaken lightly. They should have the support of a large majority of people.
9. three-fourths, or 38
10. A formal amendment must be proposed and then ratified. An informal amendment is one that is assumed by the president.
11. by Supreme Court decisions, by the actions of the president or Congress, or by changing customs
12. Congress can propose an amendment and pass it with a two-thirds vote of both houses. This is a formal change.
13. Students answers will vary but should demonstrate an understanding that the constitution organizes our government and sets guidelines for how citizens are treated and the rights given to them.

Check for Understanding

1-2. The Constitution organized the government into the executive, legislative, and judicial branches.

3-4. A change to the Constitution can be proposed by a two-thirds vote of Congress or by a national convention called by two-thirds of the states.

The Constitution, Lesson 4

What Do You Know?

popular sovereignty; limited government under the rule of law; balance of powers; checks and balances; federalism

Federalism limits the power of government by dividing it between the national government and the states.

Lesson Activities

Major Principles of Government

1. Principles are basic beliefs that guide people's lives.
2. popular sovereignty: power of government comes from the people, limited government: the government can do only what the people allow it to do, rule of law: the law applies to everyone, separation of powers: the constitution assigns each branch its own task, checks and balances: ways that each branch can limit the power of the other two branches, federalism: power is divided between the national government and the states
3. by voting in elections
4. Limited government can only do what the people allow because people have the right to vote on what they do or do not want.
5. They wanted to keep any one branch of government from becoming too powerful.
6. Popular sovereignty; limited government and the rule of law; separation of powers; checks and balances; federalism

Federalism

7. The powers given to the national government by the Constitution.
8. The powers set aside for the states.
9. Two of the following: collecting taxes, borrowing money, setting up courts and prisons.
10. the Constitution
11. Popular Sovereignty – power of government comes from the people, the people's right to rule; Limited government – the government can only do what people allow it to do; It is limited by the rule of law.; Separation of powers – The Constitution assigns each branch its own tasks.; Checks and Balances – ways that the branches watch each other and keep power in check; Federalism – Power is divided between the states and federal governments and some powers are shared.

Check for Understanding

1-2. popular sovereignty; limited government under the rule of law; balance of powers; checks and balances; federalism

1-2. federal powers (enumerated), state powers (reserved) and those shared by both (concurrent)

The Bill of Rights, Lesson 1

What Do You Know?

freedom of speech, freedom of the press, freedom of religion, freedom of assembly, freedom to petition the government

Answers will vary.

Lesson Activities

Guaranteeing Civil Liberties

1. Answers will vary.
2. freedom of religion, freedom of speech, freedom of the press, freedom of assembly, freedom to petition the government
3. Through media, speech, and print, and by petitioning the government. Being free to assemble for worship or other purposes also allows for the free expression of ideas.
4. a free press tells the people about mistakes the government has made or when power is misused
5. freedom of speech, freedom of the press, freedom of religion, freedom of assembly, freedom to petition the government
6. *Religion*: the government cannot set up an official religion and people may worship in any way they wish; *Speech*: people may say what they think without fear of being punished by the government; *Press*: government may not censor the press; *Assembly*: people have the right to gather in groups for any reason as long as it is peaceful; *Petition*: people can send letters or requests to the government

Limits on Civil Liberty

7. slander is spoken, libel is written

8. Answers will vary, but students should understand that some people would not respect the rights of others. Society could become disordered and break apart.
9. Answers will vary; for example, you cannot throw a loud party because it will disrupt the community.
10. Americans do not have unlimited civil liberties. For example, they cannot interfere with the rights of others. Also, no person may speak or write in a way that directly leads to criminal acts or to efforts to overthrow the government by force.
11. Student answers will vary but may include free speech, free press, freedom of religion, freedom to petition, and freedom of assembly. It is important to protect civil liberties so that the government does not become too powerful and cause harm to the citizens. They also help protect citizens in their daily life.

Check for Understanding

1-3. freedom of religion, speech, the press, and assembly; and the right to petition the government

4-5. freedom of speech does not allow you to tell lies; freedom of religion does not mean that you have to go to church, or that you should criticize others for not having a religion; freedom of the press does not allow newspapers, media, or magazines to print lies or make up stories; freedom of assembly means that you can protest, but not riot or damage others' property or threaten them while doing so

The Bill of Rights, Lesson 2

What Do You Know?

fair legal treatment

by enforcing rights set down by the Fourth, Fifth, Sixth, and Eighth Amendments

Lesson Activities

Rights of the Accused

1. a violation of the law, a power or privilege to which one is entitled
2. Fifth Amendment
3. right to hear charges; right to a fair trial; right to witnesses; right to a lawyer
4. The Fourth Amendment affects police work. The others have to do with courts, judges, and juries.
5. Fourth Amendment: protection against searches; Fifth Amendment: due process, no self-incrimination; no double jeopardy; Sixth Amendment: right to charges, trials, witnesses, lawyer; Eighth Amendment: no excessive bail; no cruel and unusual punishments

Additional Protections

6. The courts have said that people can own guns, but that the government can regulate the sale of guns and the permission to own them.
7. the government cannot stop people from owning guns; people's rights are not limited to what is in the Bill of Rights; powers not given to the federal government belong to the states or to the people
8. It is open-ended, allowing for other rights that may not yet be thought of. The government cannot deny these rights just because they are not specified in the Constitution.
9. They reserve unnamed rights for citizens by limiting the power of the national government to only those powers specifically granted in the Constitution.
10. Ninth; limits; Seventh; soldiers; Second; control
11. *Rights of the accused* protect the rights of people accused of crimes. They include the Fourth, Fifth, Sixth, and Eighth Amendments. They guarantee their right to fair legal treatment. Rights of citizens: *Rights of citizens* include the Second (right to bear arms), Third (government cannot force citizens to house soldiers), Seventh (rights of those involved in lawsuits), Ninth (there are additional rights beyond the Bill of Rights), and Tenth (powers not given to the federal government belong to the states or people) Amendments.

Check for Understanding

1-3. police must have a search warrant; People cannot be tried for a serious offense without an indictment, cannot be tried twice for the same crime, cannot be forced to testify against themselves, must be told what the charges are, have the right to a speedy trial, have the right to a trial by jury, must be able to question witnesses, and have the right to a fair bail amounts

4-5. soldiers may not be moved into people's homes without their permission; people are allowed to keep guns in their homes; people have rights other than the ones directly mentioned in the Bill of Rights; people can sue other people over disagreements; powers not given to the federal government by the Constitution belong to the states

The Bill of Rights Lesson 3

What Do You Know?

After the civil war, slavery became illegal.

Lesson Activities

Civil War Amendments

1. The Bill of Rights is an amendment to the Constitution, which was meant to protect citizens from the power of the federal government.
2. It was needed because freed slaves were still being deprived of their rights by state laws called black codes.
3. Everyone is supposed to be treated the same by the courts and the law.
4. the right to vote
5. The 13th Amendment ended slavery, which was the first step towards giving civil rights to African Americans. The 14th Amendment struck down the black codes, which made it illegal to deny African Americans rights. The 15th Amendment gave suffrage to African Americans.

Electoral Process and Voting Rights

6. to protect the civil rights of African Americans
7. It allowed voters to directly choose their senators. Before, their state representatives did the choosing for them.
8. women, residents of Washington, D.C., citizens ages 18–20
9. People no longer had to pay a tax to be able to vote.
10. Voting rights: Nineteenth, Twenty-third, Twenty-fourth; Electoral process: Twenty-sixth
11. Civil Rights: Thirteenth made slavery against the law: Fourteenth stated that all people born or naturalized in the U.S. were citizens and it protected the rights of freed slaves and tried to end black codes; Fifteenth extended voting rights to African American men; Voting Rights: Fifteenth extended voting rights to African American men; Nineteenth extended voting rights to women; Twenty-third allowed citizens of D.C. to vote; Twenty-fourth banned poll tax in order to vote; Twenty-sixth lowered voting age to 18

Check for Understanding

1-2. made slavery illegal in all states; granted the full rights of citizenship to African Americans; gave African American men the right to vote

3-5. senators now elected by the people rather than by state legislators; women given the right to vote; people in the District of Columbia given the right to vote for president and vice president; poll taxes eliminated; voting age lowered to 18

The Bill of Rights, Lesson 4

What Do You Know?

discrimination, segregation

Lesson Activities

Origins of the Civil Rights Movement

1. 1954, 1955, 1963, 1964, 1965; underline Brown v. Board of Education of Topeka, Kansas; Rosa Parks; Montgomery bus boycott; March on Washington; Civil Rights Act; Voting Rights Act
2. African Americans had to use services separate from those of white Americans, but they had to be treated equally even though they were separate.
3. Rose Parks refused to move to the back of the bus, where African Americans were supposed to sit, in Montgomery Alabama and was arrested for it.
4. legal challenges, boycotts, protests, marches, sit-ins
5. Both are peaceful forms of protest.
6. 1954 Brown v. Board of Education of Topeka, Kansas; 1955 Montgomery bus boycott; 1963 March on Washington; 1964 Civil Rights Act; 1965 Voting Rights Act.
7. 9 years

The Struggle Continues

8. women, Mexican Americans, Native Americans
9. Answers will vary, but students may say that such a program could give an advantage to women and minorities for example, it could result in reverse discrimination.
10. The many different groups were trying to end discrimination and gain a country that treated all its citizens with equality.
11. The Equal Rights Amendment said that no state could deny any person equal rights because of gender.
12. The Civil Rights Movement: fight against discrimination, Jim Crow laws, and segregation. Brown v. Board of Education ruled segregation unconstitutional. Martin Luther King, Jr. led the movement and boycotts spread through the South. The Civil Rights Act banned segregation in public places and outlawed job hiring discrimination.

Check for Understanding

1-3. Supreme Court decision in Brown v. Board of Education; Rosa Parks's arrest; Montgomery bus boycott; lunch counter sit-ins; Freedom Riders' voter registration drive; Martin Luther King, Jr.'s March on Washington

4-5. women; Native Americans; Mexican Americans; people with disabilities

The Legislative Branch, Lesson 1

What Do You Know?

Congress has 535 voting members.

Congress gives bills to be looked at to the many small committees that are part of Congress instead of having Congress as a whole look at all the bills.

Lesson Activities

The Two Houses of Congress

1. The Senate has two senators per state. The number of House representatives is proportional to a state's population.
2. House: 435 members; this is based on the population of the state. Senate: 100 members; every state has only two senators
3. The opinion expressed is that gerrymandering is not an activity honest lawmakers take part in.
4. 435 in the House, 100 in the Senate
5. The majority party is the party that holds more than half the seats. The other party is called the minority party.
6. Speaker of the House
7. *Pro tempore* means "for now."
8. assistant leaders that help the majority and minority leaders and make sure legislators are present for votes; the leader of the party that does not hold the majority in each house and push bills along and try to win votes

The Committee System

9. standing committees, select committees, and joint committees
10. a select committee
11. The seniority system gives the best committee assignments and chairmanships to those members who have served in Congress the longest.
12. Answers will vary but may include: Congress: Senate, House of Representatives; make laws, elected by the people of each state; represent the states, they gather for two sessions per Congress; majority party; minority party; the leader of the House is the Speaker of the House; the leader of the Senate is the President of the Senate; president pro tempore.
    Committees: review bills; they can kill or approve bills to go to Congress, they are small groups of Congress members, standing, select, joint

Check for Understanding

1-2. House of Representatives; Senate

3-5. Standing committee – permanent committees; select committee – temporary, handles special issues; joint committee – includes members from both houses and works on specific issues

The Legislative Branch, Lesson 2

What Do You Know?

Congress may not pass laws that go against the Constitution, favor one state over another, tax exports, tax businesses between states, block the writ of habeas corpus, pass bills of attainder, or pass ex post facto laws.

Congress can override the president's decisions or impeach the president.

Lesson Activities

Legislative Powers

1. Answers may include: pass laws, coin money, regulate commerce.
2. Expressed powers are listed in the Constitution, while implied powers are not. They are simply pointed to by the expressed powers.
3. raising and spending money
4. The clause is called "elastic" because it enables Congress to stretch, or expand, its powers.

Other Powers and Limits

5. propose amendments, approve president's appointments, impeach federal officials.
6. Students might refer to the injustice or unfairness of punishing someone for doing something that was legal at the time he or she did it.
7. Answers may include: Congress may not favor one state over another, tax exports, tax businesses between states.
8. Expressed powers are those clearly listed in the Constitution. Implied powers are those that are not stated specifically in the

Constitution. Checks and balances are rules and procedures built into the Constitution to keep each part of the government from gaining too much power over the others.

Check for Understanding

1-2. make laws; coin money; declare war; raise and spend money; manage commerce; raise an army; set up post offices; grant copyrights and patents

3-4. Supreme Court can declare laws unconstitutional; President can veto a bill

The Legislative Branch, Lesson 3

What Do You Know?

To be in the Senate, a person must be at least 30 years old, have been a U.S. citizen for 9 years, and be living in the state they plan to represent. To be in the House, a person must be at least 25, have been a citizen for 7 years, and are living in the state they plan to represent.

Congress also spends time on casework and trying to raise federal money for local public works called pork-barrel projects.

Lesson Activities

Qualifications and Staffing

1. age, residency, U.S. citizenship
2. The franking privilege might enable members to stay in close contact with voters.
3. *Immunity* means that a senator or representative has legal protection in certain situations.
4. lobbyists
5. research information

Congress at Work

6. Answers may vary such as: helping voters to understand laws, finding a late Social Security check. Casework is important because legislators need to support the people they represent and help them deal with the federal government.
7. Answers will vary, but should be supported. Students who think they are a good idea might suggest that they are fair rewards for outstanding representatives. Other students might suggest that an even distribution is more fair.
8. Benefits: franking, salary, free parking, office space, and trips, special medical clinic, immunity, personal staff; Qualifications: senators must be at least 30 years old, live in the state they represent, and have been a U.S. citizen for at least nine years. Those in the House must be at least 25 years old, live in the state they represent, and have been a U.S. citizen for at least seven years. The reverse tabs will vary, but students should demonstrate an understanding of the benefit they chose.

Check for Understanding

1-2. make laws, do casework, try to get federal money for projects in their state or district

The Legislative Branch, Lesson 4

What Do You Know?

Congress votes on private laws that have to do with one person or place and public laws that have to do with everyone.

A bill can be amended while it is in committee.

Lesson Activities

Types of Bills

1. private and public
2. formal statements of lawmakers' opinions or decisions: many do not have the power of law

From Bill to Law

3. pass the bill, make changes in the bill and suggest that it be passed, replace it with a new bill on the same subject, ignore the bill and let it die, also called "pigeonholing," or kill the bill by a majority vote
4. Members will argue the pros and cons and consider amendments. The House allows amendments only if they are directly related to the subject of the bill. The Senate allows its members to attach riders, or completely unrelated amendments, to a bill. Senators can speak as long as they wish about a bill, while in the House there is a time limit.
5. bill is introduced, standing committee considers bill, floor debate, vote
6. members say "aye" or "no" to a bill
7. Answers will vary. Generally, riders are viewed as ways to sneak items into a law.
8. Bill is introduced – a bill comes to Congress for consideration as a law; bill goes to a committee – subcommittees of Congress review and research the bill and recommend a course of action; bill is debated in Congress – if the bill goes to Congress, members will debate its pros and cons; Congress votes on the bill – members vote whether to make it a law

Check for Understanding

1-2. citizens, the president, special-interest groups

3-4. pass the bill on to the full House or Senate for a vote; vote to kill the bill; ignore the bill and do nothing with it; make changes in the bill and suggest that the House and Senate pass it; rewrite the bill

The Executive Branch, Lesson 1

What Do You Know?

Any U.S. citizen who is at least 35 years old, was born in the United States, and has lived in the United States for 14 years can be president.

Yes, the president can be replaced before the end of a term if he or she dies, resigns, becomes seriously ill, or is removed from office.

Lesson Activities

Office of the President

1. Because the president has one of the most important jobs in America, the Constitution's rules are meant to make sure the person who is president is suitable for the job.
2. Answers will vary, some examples: John F. Kennedy, Teddy Roosevelt, George W. Bush.
3. Electoral College: The Electoral College is a group of people who cast votes for the president and vice president. There are 538 electors. Each state has the same number of electors as members of Congress. To win, a candidate must get at least half of the votes.; President: The constitution requires the president to be at least 35 years old, born in the United States, and have lived in the United States for at least 14 years. Most presidents have had similar backgrounds. The presidential election is every 4 years and one person may be elected to two consecutive terms. Vice President: The vice president serves in 4-year terms and has no specific duties. That person must be able to step up as president should the president be unable to lead. The qualifications for becoming vice president are the same as for president.
4. A candidate must get at least 270 votes to win in the Electoral College.
5. to prevent one person from becoming too powerful
6. The United States is a democracy. Giving one person too much power could put that democracy in jeopardy.

Presidential Succession

7. It is important for the nation to know who will be president if something should happen to the current president.
8. The new president picks the vice president and Congress must approve their choice.
9. Secretary of State
10. Possible examples: dies, leaves office, seriously disabled, or surgery
11. The vice presidency was left empty when the vice president had to become president.
12. President: at least 35 years old, born in the United States, and have lived in the United States for at least 14 years. Vice president: at least 35 years old, born in the United States, and have lived in the United States for at least 14 years. Presidential successor: the person who steps in as president if the president is unable to work; vice president is first, followed by the Speaker of the House, the president pro tempore of the Senate, and then the secretary of state.

Check for Understanding

1-2. must be at least 35 years old; must have been born in the United States; must have lived in the United States for the last 14 years

3-4. The new president must choose a person to be vice president and Congress must approve the decision.

The Executive Branch, Lesson 2

What Do You Know?

The president is the most powerful public official in the country, so his job is to execute the laws passed by Congress.

The president's roles are Chief Executive, Chief Diplomat, Head of State, Commander in Chief, Economic Leader, Legislative Leader, and Party Leader.

Lesson Activities

Presidential Powers

1. The power of the president to reject bills passed by Congress.
2. execute the laws passed by Congress; veto bills; call Congress into special session; serve as commander in chief; receive leaders and other officials of foreign countries; make treaties (with Senate approval); appoint various top government officials (with Senate approval); pardon people convicted of federal crimes

3. The purpose of the State of the Union speech is to tell Congress how the country is doing.
4. Has veto power, pardons or reduces penalties for federal crimes, names top government officials, makes treaties, receives foreign leaders, serves as commander in chief, and calls special sessions of congress.

Presidential Roles

5. The president's main role is to carry out the nation's laws, which he or she does by executive orders and choosing the justices to serve on the Supreme Court and judges to serve on federal courts.
6. Students should underline the sentences "This is an important power because Supreme Court justices serve for life. That is why presidents try to choose judges who share views similar to their own."
7. A pardon forgives a crime and punishment.
8. A pardon forgives a crime and ends punishment for an individual, while amnesty is pardon for a group of people.
9. The president represents the interests of the whole nation. Members of Congress represent the interests of their states or congressional districts.
10. Answers will vary but students must be persuasive and clear on their reasons.
11. B. 1-2. represents the United States government to other countries, appoints ambassadors
C. 1-2. represents the American people, greets visiting leaders from other countries, gives out medals at ceremonies
D. 1-2. allows president to back up foreign policy decisions with force when needed, has the power to order troops into battle
E. 1-2. is expected to find solutions to unemployment, high taxes, and rising prices. Plans the federal budget each year.
F. 1-2. gives Congress ideas for new laws, works with Congress to get laws passes, makes speeches around the country to get citizens to support new laws being passed.
G. 1-2. supports other party members running for office and helps the party raise money
12. It limits the president's power to send troops into combat.
13. Powers: carries out laws, veto bills, call Congress into special session, serves a commander in chief, names top government officials, receives dignitaries, pardons or reduces the penalties against people convicted of federal crimes. Roles: chief executive, diplomat, head of state, commander in chief, party leader, legislative leader, economic leader

Check for Understanding

1-3. veto bills passed by Congress; send troops into battle; make treaties; call special sessions of Congress; pardon or reduce the sentences of people convicted of federal crimes

4-5. chief executive; commander in chief of the military; chief diplomat; head of state

The Executive Branch, Lesson 3

What Do You Know?

Foreign policy is the plan a nation follows when it deals with other nations.

The government makes foreign policy so it can prioritize various dealings with other countries.

Lesson Activities

The President and Foreign Policy

1. because trade creates markets for American goods and jobs for American workers
2. national security
3. the State Department, Defense Department, National Security Council, Office of the Director of National Intelligence, and Central Intelligence Agency
4. Only Congress can declare war, but because the Constitution is not clear about how the branches of government should work together, the war powers shifts between Congress and the president.

The Tools of Foreign Policy

5. an agreement between the president and the leader of another country
6. Students should underline *The president appoints ambassadors, but the appointments must be approved, or confirmed, by the Senate.*
7. foreign aid
8. embargos, sanctions, tariffs
9. Foreign Policy: definition: a plan a nation follows to deal with other countries; goals: national security, trade, peace, democracy; President tools: make treaties, executive agreement, use of ambassadors, recognition of other governments, foreign aid, trade sanctions, embargos, military force; Congress tools: approve treaties and ambassadors, tariffs, decides participation in international groups

Check for Understanding

1-2. protect the nation; promote trade; promote peace; encourage democracy

3-5. treaties, executive agreements, foreign aid, trade sanctions, trade embargos, military force, selection of ambassadors

The Executive Branch, Lesson 4

What Do You Know?

The executive office directs the White House staff, handles the president's schedule, helps to prepare the federal budget, monitors other agencies' spending, helps the president with defense and security, and helps the president carry out the responsibilities of the executive branch.

The president's cabinet is the heads of 15 executive departments and these heads advise the president and manage the work of their departments.

Lesson Activities

Executive Office Agencies

1. President Franklin D. Roosevelt
2. the chief of staff
3. Answers will vary but should show an understanding of what the Secretary of State does.
4. Council of Economic Advisors: helps the president as economic leader, National Security Council: helps the president with defense and security, Office of Management and Budget: works with the president to prepare the federal budget and monitors how government agencies spend their money

The President's Cabinet

5. whenever the president decides it is necessary
6. the terrorist attacks of September 11, 2001
7. Answers will vary but should show an understanding of how presidential cabinet departments advise the president.
8. issues related to commerce

The Federal Bureaucracy

9. the hundreds of agencies below the cabinet departments are known as the federal bureaucracy
10. make new laws work, carry out the government's daily work, regulate various types of business public services, and public utilities
11. executive agencies, government corporations, regulatory commissions
12. Students should underline this sentence in the regulatory commissions paragraph: "These are the only independent agencies that do not have to report to the president."
13. The merit system is a system that is based on a person's abilities. The people take a test and are hired depending on the skills the tests have shown.
14. the top-level jobs in a department or agency
15. The EOP is the president and the people and agencies that report to the president. Its purpose is to help the president carry out his/her duties. It includes the White House staff, OMB, NSC, CEA, and other agencies. The Cabinet are the heads of various departments who are the president's closest advisors. Its purpose is to communicate issues to the president and advise him/her on problems facing the nation.

Check for Understanding

1-2. Office of Management and Budget, National Security Council, Office of Administration

3-4. People in the president's cabinet manage their departments and advise the president on important matters

The Judicial Branch, Lesson 1

What Do You Know?

The federal courts make sure the laws are enforced fairly and interpret the law.

Criminal and civil cases

Lesson Activities

Role of the Federal Courts

1. make sure laws are enforced fairly and interpret the law
2. between two private parties; between a private party and the government; between federal and state or local governments
3. The Framers wanted to guarantee that people would receive equal justice in all the states.
4. District courts heard minor civil and criminal cases. Circuit courts heard more serious cases and appeals.
5. It is a legal system that has both federal and state courts.
6. The federal courts exist to make sure citizens in every state are treated the same.
7. Supreme Court, appeals or circuit courts, district courts

Federal Court Jurisdiction

8. the authority to hear and decide cases
9. Any two: cases involving constitutional rights or federal law, disputes between states, cases involving admiralty or maritime law, cases involving the federal government, cases involving foreign governments, cases involving U.S. diplomats
10. Federal: a crime committed at sea; State: a lawsuit between citizens of the same state; Both: a case involving a crime that broke both state and federal laws.
11. Federal exclusive jurisdiction is reserved for cases that only the federal courts can hear and decide such as cases related to the Constitution, federal laws, disputes between states, between citizens of different states, the federal government, foreign governments and treaties, incidents at sea, and diplomats. Concurrent jurisdiction is reserved for cases that both federal and state courts can hear and decide. These mostly involve crimes that break both federal and state laws. State exclusive jurisdiction is reserved for cases that can be heard and decided by state courts. These involve only state laws.

Check for Understanding

1-2. civil cases, criminal cases
3. Cases involving the Constitution, federal laws, disputes between states, disputes between citizens of different states, foreign governments and treaties, accidents or crimes at sea, disputes between U.S. and foreign governments

The Judicial Branch, Lesson 2

What Do You Know?

district courts, appeals courts, Supreme Court

Judges are appointed by the president with the Senate's consent.

Lesson Activities

The Lower Courts

1. District courts have original jurisdiction; i.e., hear cases for the first time. Appeals courts have appellate jurisdiction; i.e., review rulings in cases
2. Appeals courts uphold decisions of lower courts, reverse decisions of lower courts, or send cases back to lower courts for retrial.
3. The opinion explains the legal thinking behind the court's decision. The opinion is also an example to be followed by other judges
4. Precedents are powerful legal arguments that help guide future decisions.
5. A lawsuit is a legal action in which a person or group sues to collect damages for some harm that is done. Litigants are people involved in a lawsuit.

Federal Judges

6. They are appointed by the president and approved by the Senate.
7. The Senate giving consent to the presidential appointments is a "check" on the executive office.
8. Magistrate judges issue search and arrest warrants, hear preliminary evidence, and try minor cases.
9. Federal Judges: appointed by the president, serve for life, removed only by impeachment, 650 federal judges in the district courts, appeals court has 6-28 judges, the Sup-eme court has nine justices. Appointment: federal judges are appointed by the president and then approved by the Senate. The practice of appointment is called senatorial courtesy, where the senators from the nominee's home state are told about the nominee, and if they don't like them the president will choose someone else. This does not apply to appeals court judges or Supreme Court justices. Tenure: Federal judges have tenure, which means they can't be fired, so if they have to make difficult decisions they do not have to fear losing their job. Support Staff: District courts have magistrates that help judges with routine work, issuing search and arrest warrants, and hearing preliminary evidence.

Check for Understanding

1-3. district courts, appeals courts, Supreme Court
4-5. must be nominated by the president and approved by the Senate

The Judicial Branch, Lesson 3

What Do You Know?

Appeals from lower courts, cases involving diplomats from other countries, and cases involving disputes between states

Judicial review

Lesson Activities

Jurisdiction and Duties

1. appeals from the lower courts
2. The ruling of the lower court stands.

Power and Limits

3. The Supreme Court: the final authority in all cases involving the Constitution, acts of Congress, and treaties with other countries; original jurisdiction in cases involving diplomats from other countries and disputes between states; deals with mostly appealed cases; have the power of judicial review and nullifying a law. Judicial Review: the power to review any federal, state, or local law or action to see if it is constitutional. Opinion: explains the legal thinking behind the court's decision. The opinion is also an example to be followed by other judges.
4. legislative branch, or Congress
5. It means that it does not follow what is in the Constitution and is therefore not allowed.
6. 1789: judicial review over state laws; 1803: judicial review over laws passed by Congress
7. It can pass a new law. It can amend an unconstitutional law. It can try to amend the Constitution.
8. The Supreme Court relies on the executive branch and the states to obey and enforce its rulings. The legislative branch, or Congress, decides how the Supreme Court should be organized and what its powers should be.
9. It gives the U.S. Supreme Court the power to review state laws to make sure they are in keeping with the Constitution as the supreme law of the nation.
10. Kinds of Cases: cases involving the Constitution, acts of Congress, and treaties with other countries; original jurisdiction over cases that involved diplomats from other countries and disputes between states, most cases are appealed cases. Powers: judicial review, nullifying laws. Limits: Congress can change unconstitutional laws, court cannot enforce its rulings, court can only rule on cases that come to it through the courts.

Check for Understanding

1-3. all cases involving the Constitution; acts of Congress; treaties

4-5. Power of judicial review; power to nullify, or cancel, any law it rules unconstitutional

The Judicial Branch, Lesson 4

What Do You Know?

The Supreme Court makes sure laws stay constitutional in changing social conditions and that the people's constitutional rights are protected.

Justices study briefs that lawyers from both sides have presented and ask questions, as well as listen to oral arguments. Then they meet to make decisions in a secret meeting and a majority vote decides the case.

Lesson Activities

Court Procedures

1. Justices look for cases involving constitutional questions; real people and events; and cases that affect the whole country, rather than one person or group.
2. the decision of the lower court stands
3. Four of the nine justices must agree to hear a case for it to appear on the docket.

How the Court's Rulings Are Made

4. what most justices think and why, the view of justices who disagree with the majority, the view of justices who agree with the majority but for different reasons, the view held by all the justices
5. Answers will vary but should have the same main idea as the text.
6. Brown v. Board of Education (1954), Tinker v. Des Moines (1969), Hazelwood v. Kuhlmeier (1988)
7. Answers will vary but should illustrate an understanding of the case and it's impact on life in the United States.
8. Answers will vary but should illustrate an understanding of the term and its importance.
9. Social conditions can influence the Court to reinterpret the law and overrule precedents.
10. Types of cases they hear: raise constitutional questions, deal with real people and events, affect the whole country not just one person or group; Types of written opinions: concurring opinions agree with the decision but for different reasons; dissenting opinions oppose the decision; unanimous opinion when all justices vote the same way

Check for Understanding

1-3. cases involving freedom of speech, freedom of religion, freedom of the press, right to a fair trial, voting rights, or anything involving the Constitution and how it is applied

4-6. majority, concurring, dissenting, unanimous

Political Parties, Lesson 1

What Do You Know?

Political parties help us communicate with the government.

The Democratic Party thinks that government should help fix society's problems. The Republican Party thinks that government should not get involved.

Lesson Activities

Growth of American Parties

1. Democratic and Republican
2. Students should underline *because people had different ideas about what the government should do.*
3. late 1790's, 1828–1830, 1854
4. the Democratic Party and the Whig Party
5. Federalists believed a strong national government was needed to protect the rights of individuals and to build a strong economy.
6. people who were against slavery

Third Parties

7. parties that form to compete with the Democratic and Republican parties
8. Both are single-issue parties.
9. farmers and laborers; because they wanted direct democracy and to have an eight-hour work day
10. getting on the ballot is difficult, low funds, weak networks
11. Third parties can be single-issue, formed around a particular cause; ideological, based on a political philosophy; or formed to support a strong, independent leader.

Party Differences

12. *The platform gives the party's positions on important issues. It also states the party's basic beliefs.*
13. Both parties moderate their views to appeal to as many voters as possible and to reach the majority of American people.
14. *Democrats*: want government to fix society's problems; large active government *Republicans*: promote free market to fix society's problems; little government interaction in personal lives; *Third Parties*: usually surround a person, a belief, or an issue

Check for Understanding

1-2. the Federalist Party and the Democratic-Republican Party

3-4. to promote a single issue that is especially important to them; for ideological reasons; to support a strong, independent candidate; to support a new idea that has not yet caught on with the major parties

Political Parties, Lesson 2

What Do You Know?

Political parties organize people to help candidates get elected.

Candidates are nominated in primary elections.

Lesson Activities

Organization of Political Parties

1. delegates from every state
2. A caucus is a meeting of state and local party members. A precinct is a defined area in which voters live.
3. *National*: The national committee is in charge of the party and organizes the national convention. It includes people from every state. *State, County, Local*: These help local candidates win elections, support the national party, and support their party's choice for president and vice president.
4. High-level party leaders depend on precinct leaders to build the local party, to organize volunteer efforts, to get out information about party issues, and to get voters to the polls.
5. Student answers will vary, but they should indicate that having one party with all the power could lead to corruption and trouble, such as having only certain people receive assistance.

Selecting Party Candidates

6. To nominate someone means to choose a person to be a candidate.
7. the Democratic Party and the Republican Party
8. In an open primary, voters do not need to declare a party preference in order to vote for the party's nominees. In a closed primary, voters must declare a party affiliation before being allowed to vote for the party's nominees.

Other Political Party Functions

9. Student answers will vary, but could include keeping people informed of issues, providing a link between government and the people, and speaking for the people.
10. Political parties help get people to the polls on Election Day.

11. Student answers will vary, but should demonstrate that they understand that by watching elected officials closely we can be more assured that they are acting ethically and in the best interests of the public.
12. The parties help citizens communicate with the government and make sure that the government remains responsive to the people.
13. Student answers will vary but should demonstrate an understanding of the value of political parties and how they help citizens and government work together.

Check for Understanding

1-3. Any three: state, county, local, wards, precincts

4-5. Any two: closed primary, open primary, petition

Voting and Elections, Lesson 1

What Do You Know?

go to a polling place and cast a ballot

Voting is a right and a responsibility that helps count towards making decisions in the government and having a say in the community, state, or nation.

Lesson Activities

Qualifying to Vote

1. a formal change
2. the Nineteenth Amendment
3. To be eligible means that a person is allowed to vote, or meets the necessary requirements.
4. A person must be age 18 or older and be a U.S. citizen to vote.

steps in the Voting Process

5. driver's license, birth certificate, or another form of identification that proves age and citizenship
6. The National Voter Registration Act is meant to get more people to register to vote, and hopefully it has meant that more people have registered, especially when they turn 18.
7. registering, preparing, and casting a ballot
8. At a polling place, you show a form of identification and then enter a booth to vote using a ballot.
9. paper ballot
10. In 2000 the Supreme Court ruled the ballots should not be recounted, meaning George W. Bush won the election.

Why Your Vote Counts

11. Every citizen's vote is counted in the same way, with the same value, as every other citizen's vote.
12. Answers will vary.
13. This means that 50 percent of eligible voters actually voted. Or, that 50 percent of the people who could have voted did not vote.
14. *Voting Rights*: Student answers will vary but should demonstrate an understanding that to have the ability to vote gives citizens the ability to govern themselves and control the power of the government in their lives.
    Voting Requirements: a person must be 18 years old, have lived in a state for a certain period of time, and be a U.S. citizen

Check for Understanding

1-2. be eighteen years old; a United States citizen

3-5. have proper identification with you, register, find a polling place

Voting and Elections, Lesson 2

What Do You Know?

primary election, general election, initiative election, referendum, recall election

Lesson Activities

Types of Elections

1. Primary election: picks candidates for the general election; General election: candidates get elected to office; Initiative election: to vote on an issue; Referendum: to accept or reject a law passed by state legislature; Recall election: vote to remove someone from office
2. because it would be difficult to get anything done in Congress if all the Senators were elected at the same time
3. They can try to get the change enacted through the initiative process.
4. In a recall election, voters can remove a person from office, while a special election is used to find their replacement.

Presidential Elections

5. the members of the Electoral College
6. candidate B
7. A campaign is the efforts made by a person trying to win an election.

Running for Office

8. Answers will vary.

9. This means they go from door to door to gather support. They also make telephone calls and send e-mails to tell people about their candidate.
10. Candidates want endorsements to gain the favor of voters who like or admire the person or organization giving the endorsement.
11. They are set up by interest groups to raise money for candidates.
12. to make rules about how much money candidates can spend on their campaigns
13. Answers will vary and may include that the Electoral College is used to elect the president and vice president, as opposed to direct voters electing them; there is debate whether it is useful and fair; the number of electors for each state matches that state's congressional seats; it is a winner-take-all system; and it is required by the Constitution.

Check for Understanding

1-2. Primary elections, general elections, initiatives, referendums, recall elections
3. It is required by the Constitution.
4-5. Answers will vary, and may include, announcing that he or she is running for office, giving speeches and interviews, holding debates, and trying to appeal to as many voters as possible.

Public Opinion and Government, Lesson 1

What Do You Know?

Public opinion includes the ideas and views of the people about an issue or a person.

Public opinion can be measured with public opinion polls and election results

Lesson Activities

Public Opinion

1. a personal judgment about a person or thing
2. the ideas and views of the people about an issue or a person
3. a person's background, mass media, interest groups, age, gender, race, income, religion, occupation, or place of residency
4. Answers will vary, but one of the following should be circled: television, radio, newspapers, movies, recordings, Web sites, or books.
5. The three features of public opinion are direction, intensity, and stability. *Polls*: Political leaders look at polls to help them make laws that fit the people's needs. They also look at polls to try to win elections. *Public Opinion*: Elected representatives must understand how the public feels on key issues so they know the will of the people.
6. Answers will vary but should show an understanding of public opinion.

Public Opinion Polls

7. a public opinion poll
8. A good sample is a smaller version of the U.S. population that reflects the opinions of people all over the country.
9. Students should underline, "by chance," and "a person who conducts a poll."
10. Its questions wi l be worded to try to influence your response.
11. Polls can help the government know the opinion of the people on a certain issue, but others say polls distract leaders, unfairly affect election results, and can sway voters not to vote.
12. *Policy* is proposed decisions or actions taken to solve problems. *Opinion* is a personal judgment about a person or thing.

Check for Understanding

1-2. joining an interest group or participating in a public opinion poll
3-4. A democratic government is ruled by the people through their elected representatives. In order for those representatives to know the will of the people, they must understand how the public feels on the key issues of the day. The government looks at public opinion to decide which types of programs the people will support.

Public Opinion and Government, Lesson 2

What Do You Know?

newspapers, magazines, books, the Internet, television, radio

Answers may vary, but possible answer might be: No, freedom of the press should not be limited because the press watches over government activities for the people, spreads ideas, tests public opinion for politicians, and keeps the people informed.

Lesson Activities

The Influence of the Media

1. print and electronic
2. Politicians need media coverage to get their message out. Reporters need information to write stories.

3. secretly pass
4. It helps the public by exposing wrongdoing. Acting as a watchdog helps the media by uncovering stories that attract large audiences.
5. by deciding who can use the airwaves and by punishing stations that break the rules

Protecting the Press

6. In order for something to be considered libel, it must be proven that the publisher of the information knew the information was wrong and therefore published it with evil intent.
7. Freedoms: The government cannot use prior restraint, the press can write whatever they want, and many states have shield laws to protect press sources. Restrictions: cannot publish libel

Check for Understanding

1. By choosing which stories to cover, the media influence where the public's attention will be focused and provide the government with public feedback on issues.
2. The government does not allow libel. It also regulates the airwaves.

Public Opinion and Government, Lesson 3

What Do You Know?

Special interest groups are interest groups that work for special causes, like the Sierra Club works to protect nature.

Interest groups help to raise money for candidates that support their interests and try to shape government policy.

Lesson Activities

Interest Groups

1. Answers will vary. Students should address the people's right to join together over certain issues to influence the government.
2. The American Federation of Labor and Congress of Industrial Organizations is the largest interest group for workers that focuses on wages and working conditions
3. Answers will vary. Students should support their decision.
4. nonpartisan
5. PACs, lobbyists, and propaganda
6. Lobbyists contact lawmakers on behalf of interest groups to try and convince officials to support the ideas of the interest group.
7. Answers will vary and may include, name-calling, stacked cards, glittering generalities, bandwagon, endorsement, just plain folks, and transfer.
8. endorsement

Regulating Interest Groups

9. so they cannot use friendships and inside information to help special-interest groups
10. Students should underline the sentence in the last paragraph that reads: "They think these groups have too much influence."
11. *Methods*: hire lobbyists, form political action committees to raise money for elections, issue propaganda; *Regulations*: must register, can give limited amounts of money to candidates, must share information about who they contact and how much they spend; *Purpose*: to make sure interest groups don't have too much or unfair influence in government policy

Check for Understanding

1-3. through elections, the courts, lawmakers, or by trying to shape public opinion

4-5. laws limit how much money PACs can give to candidates; lobbyists must register and report who they are working for and how much money they spend; lawmakers are not permitted to work as lobbyists for a period of time after they leave office

State Government, Lesson 1

What Do You Know?

It shares power between the federal government and the states.

Every state has a constitution and they have the same rights under the federal Constitution.

Lesson Activities

Federal and State Powers

1. a system of government in which power is divided between federal and state governments; some powers are shared
2. Students should underline, "Framers created a central government that was stronger than the central government under the Articles of Confederation. However, they also thought that states were important too."
3. Student answers might vary but could include: They must acknowledge marriages that happen in other states, One state cannot tax people from another state at a higher rate than the people of their state; Article IV section 3

4. Implied powers are derived from the expressed powers. They are the powers needed to exercise the expressed powers.
5. both governments need money to operate
6. state government
7. collect taxes, borrow money, spend for the general welfare, set up court systems, pass and enforce laws
8. States cannot declare war, issue their own money, impose taxes on imports from other countries or states, make treaties with another country, or take away the rights of citizens without due process of law.
9. It makes federal law more powerful than state law, so that if a state law conflicts, it gets thrown out.
10. An unfunded mandate forces states to spend their own money to fulfill a federal goal that they might not share.

The State Constitutions

11. State constitutions are often longer because they are more specific.
12. *U. S. Constitution*: gives the power to coin money; president is commander-in-chief of the armed forces; can buy land from another country; *Both*: divide government into legislative, executive, and judicial branches; define the powers of the three branches; include a bill of rights; include a process for amending the constitution; *State Constitutions*: every state has one; tend to be very specific; some are quite long

Check for Understanding

1-2. power to tax, borrow money, pass and enforce laws, establish courts, spend for the general welfare

3-4. Any two of the following: create three branches, define powers of each branch, include bill of rights, amendment process, processes for forming local governments

State Government, Lesson 2

What Do You Know?

make laws, vote to approve governor's choices for state offices, help citizens in the district

States have to always have a balanced budget, so it can be hard on states when there are economic problems. They rely only on sales taxes and income taxes for money, so they have a far greater challenge than a town, city, or county.

Lesson Activities

How Legislatures Function

1. Bicameral means the legislature has two houses, while unicameral has only one house.
2. The Speaker is the leader of the lower house and is chosen by members of the house. The lieutenant governor usually heads the senate and then the members of each party choose a leader, who become the majority and minority leaders.
3. The federal government conducts a census every ten years so that districts can be redrawn to reflect changes in population.
4. students should underline, "having unfair district sizes"
5. making laws
6. Students shoulc circle Step 2.
7. Nebraska; its legislature is unicameral
8. They can petition for a popular referendum on the question of whether to repeal the law.

State Economic Issues

9. income taxes and sales tax
10. When people lose jobs, they make less money and buy fewer things. States collect less income and sales taxes. At the same time, hard times mean that people need more services from the state, not less.
11. *Income*: sales tax, income tax, fees charged for various things; *Spending*: aid to local governments, benefits to the poor and disabled, salaries of state workers, health care, schools, police, roads, parks; *Financial Challenges*: When the economy is bad, paying for these services is difficult. States collect less in income tax and sales tax. More people need help from the government.

Check for Understanding

1-3. make laws, vote to approve a governor's choices for state offices, help the citizens in their district

4-6. any three: aid to local governments, benefits to the poor and the disabled, state employee salaries, services such as health care, schools, police, roads, parks

State Government, Lesson 3

What Do You Know?

heads the executive branch, writes the budget, is a party leader, sends bills to legislature, appoints judges

State executive departments carry out laws, oversee elections, record state laws, keep track of the money the state collects and spends, oversee the state's public school system.

Lesson Activities

The Governor

1. Some things that governors do are because it is the custom, not because the law says they have to. The law does not say the governor has to be the party's leader, but it is the custom for him or her to be.
2. Both head the executive branch; both carry out laws, head the military, and appoint people to fill executive branch positions.
3. The state senate must often approve the choice before it becomes final.
4. veto power
5. Answers might include: party leader, ceremonial leader, head of executive branch, commander of state militia, fills vacant Senate seat, signs/vetoes laws, appoints judges

State Executive Departments

6. If the official is elected, he or she may be more independent than if the governor had appointed him or her.
7. The secretary of state oversees elections and keeps track of state laws. He or she also keeps track of official records.
8. He or she is the state's lawyer and represents the state in legal matters.
9. Cabinets give the governor advice and share information and special knowledge on issues.
10. Answers will vary but students could share that the governor heads the executive branch, makes sure laws are carried out, heads state's National Guard, fills various state positions, writes budgets, can send bills to the legislature, can veto all or part of a bill, appoints judges, pardons criminals, and commutes sentences.

Check for Understanding

1-3. heads the executive branch; responsible for carrying out the state's laws; heads the state's National Guard; appoints some state officials and judges; can choose a replacement for U.S. Senate if the seat is vacated

4-5. secretary of state, attorney general, state treasurer, state auditor, commissioner or superintendent of education

State Government, Lesson 4

What Do You Know?

In a state judicial system, there are trial courts, appellate courts, and then state supreme courts.

Answers will vary.

Lesson Activities

The Structure of State Courts

1. to separate minor cases that can be handled quickly from serious cases that take more time and resources
2. Panels of judges hear appeals from lower courts.
3. the plaintiff is the one claiming harm; the defendant is the one said to have harmed the plaintiff
4. a higher-level trial court
5. lower court, appellate court
6. to hear the appeals from the intermediate appellate courts
7. Either personal bias or the pressure to be popular with voters could sway a judge's decision.

Staffing the Courts

8. Answers will vary but should include an understanding that a judge needs to be fair and impartial. They should not allow their personal beliefs or politics to affect the decisions that they hand down in matters of law.
9. by the governor, legislature, state supreme court, city officials
10. by election or by the governor's appointment
11. A board can look into the complaints about the judges, and if they find the judge's actions were wrong, it can recommend to the state supreme court that the judge be disciplined. That court has the power to remove the judge.
12. *Qualifications*: Judges must know the law, be free of bias, and be independent. *Appointment or Election:* Judges may be appointed by the governor, the legislature, the state supreme court, or city officials. Other judges are elected by the voters. *Removal from Office*: Judges can be impeached, but most states have a board that can suggest removal to the state supreme court. The court has the power to suspend or remove the judge.

Check for Understanding

1-2. the lower court it is the trial court; the higher court is the appellate court

3. election

4. appointed by governor

Local Government, Lesson 1

What Do You Know?

They both provide public services.

Local governments provide public services and officials keep everything in order.

Lesson Activities

How City Governments are Created

1. police and fire protection, water and sewer service, schools, public transportation, and libraries
2. by applying for and receiving a city charter from the state legislature or by the city writing its own charter under home rule
3. federal and state grants; taxes; fees and fines

The Mayor-Council Form

4. the mayor-council form, the council-manager form, the commission form
5. separation of powers
6. A strong mayor, acting in an executive role, dominates city government.
7. because responsibility is in many hands and depends on people working well together

Council-Manager and Commission Governments

8. It was seen as a way to make city government more honest and well-organized.
9. Council-manager: Executive powers go to a hired city manager, and a council has the legislative power. Commission: Executive and legislative power are both held by the commissioners, each of whom heads a department.
10. a lack of leadership; this form of government encourages commissioners to focus on their departments at the expense of the city as a whole.
11. mayor-council system; strong-mayor system; weak-mayor system; council-manager system; commission system
12. a city and its surrounding suburbs and small towns
13. *Council-manager*: elected city council hires the manager, council can fire the manager, government divided by legislative and executive; popular form of government organization; *Both*: oversee departments and budgets; *Commission*: the council of department heads runs the city, less-used form of government organization

Check for Understanding

1-3. any three: police, fire, water supply, schools, libraries, transportation

4-6. mayor-council, council-manager, and commission

7-8. make executive decisions, write the budget, veto laws passed by council, appoint department heads, oversee departments like police and fire

Local Government, Lesson 2

What Do You Know?

County governments have a board of three to five members called commissioners that acts as legislature and sometimes has both legislative and executive power.

County government solves local problems, like sewer and water service, police and fire protection, road repairs, and public transportation. They also look into crimes and bring charges against people suspected of breaking the law.

Lesson Activities

How County Governments Are Organized

1. *Counties*: more than 3,000 in the nation, Alaska calls them boroughs and Louisiana calls them parishes; within each county is a county seat; all towns in that county are within a 1-day journey and back on horse; the population varies
2. They were chosen to be accessible to county residents. In the Midwest and South, that included being able to travel back and forth by horse and buggy in one day.

The Functions of County Government

3. Many county governments have taken over the duties of city governments.
4. It means to demand and collect the tax from people; commissioners
5. a board of three to five elected commissioners or supervisors
6. Commission-manager: The board of commissioners appoints a manager who handles the day-to-day operations of government. The board functions as a legislature. Commission-executive: A county executive is elected by the voters to make executive and administrative decisions. The board serves as a legislative body. Strong commission: Three to five commissioners are elected by the voters to handle all aspects of administering county government.
7. they are elected by voters

8. The county assessor's estimate of the value of land is used to figure out property tax.

9. Answers will vary. Examples include: the condition of the buildings or property, whether it is used for business or residence, location, and size

10. County governments help citizens by providing many local services such as sewer, water, roads, transportation, police, and fire services. They also handle local court cases.

Check for Understanding

1-3. strong commission consisting of 3 to 5 elected officials; commission-manager; commission-elected executive

4-5. sewer and water services, road repair, police and fire protection, public transportation

Local Government, Lesson 3

What Do You Know?

We need town governments to deal with very specific local problems.

Town meetings are held in towns, where they discuss local and world issues, and vote on town rules, taxes, and budgets. They often have representatives at these meetings now, where before they had open town meetings to include everyone in the town. In villages people elect an executive to run their government.

Lesson Activities

Towns and Town Meetings

1. A unit smaller than a city but bigger than a village is called a town in the New England area, and called a township in other areas, like the Midwest.

2. They discuss local and world issues and vote on town rules, taxes, and budgets. Citizens, not elected representatives, make the decisions.

3. When government gets more complex, town meetings, i.e., direct democracy, does not always work well.

4. Answers will vary. Examples include: building a new school or town hall, budget concerns, and new laws or taxes

Townships and Villages

5. They kept the original township borders set by Congress.

6. Voters elect a board or committee to pass ordinances and do the township's business.

7. Both villages and cities must get permission from the state to organize their local governments.

8. better services; improves community status and makes it more attractive to potential new residents and businesses; more self-government

9. *Direct democracy*: All voters help make decisions and discuss issues. *Representative*: Voters elect officials to run the government and make decisions.

Check for Understanding

1-2. town rules, taxes, and a budget

3-4. elected board, an elected executive, or a hired city manager

Dealing with Community Issues, Lesson 1

What Do You Know?

the government's response to solving problems or resolving issues in the community

Local governments use planning commissions to make policy.

Lesson Activities

Shaping Public Policy

1. Circle: transportation, clean water, good schools; Underline: lack housing, overcrowding in schools, need more businesses

2. the government's response to solving problems or resolving issues in the community

3. when they are dealing with a local government

Planning for the Future

4. Each has a different interest and brings a different perspective to the planning process.

5. Answers will vary. Example: conservation efforts

6. A community should consider infrastructure. People and businesses depend on it for daily survival and economic activity. Without it, a community could not function. A community should also consider its resources.

7. priorities and resources

8. *Short term plan*: carried out within a few years; *Both*: help the future, affect many people; *Long-term plan*: takes 10-20 years or more to complete

Check for Understanding

1. short-term
2. long-term
3. short-term

Dealing with Community Issues, Lesson 2

What Do You Know?

low test scores, high dropout rates, crime and violence, lack of funding

States are trying new methods like charter schools and tuition vouchers.

Lesson Activities

Public Education

1. with local taxes and state money
2. It provides funds for schools and sets down rules.
3. Wealthy districts have high property taxes, which generates more revenue that schools can use.
4. low test scores, high dropout rates, crime and violence, lack of funding
5. schools receive state funding but do not have to meet many state regulations for public schools.
6. other choice
7. charter schools, tuition vouchers, more testing, alternative schools

Crime and Social Problems

8. It is highest in big cities because they have many poor people, and poverty is a root cause of crime.
9. In rural areas, county sheriffs and deputies enforce the law, while the state police and highway police enforce state law. Large police forces take care of the cities.
10. by reducing crime in the neighborhood, it might also reduce violence in the school
11. to fight poverty and other social problems
12. Crime: community policing, Poverty: welfare programs
13. *Local government*: runs the schools, raises money for the schools; *State government*: sets rules for education, gives money to local communities for schools; *Federal government*: sets rules for education, gives money to public schools

Check for Understanding

1-2. Local government: runs the schools, raises money for the schools; State government: sets rules for education, gives money to local communities for schools; Federal government: sets rules for education, gives money to public schools

Dealing with Community Issues, Lesson 3

What Do You Know?

air pollution, water pollution, land pollution

factories, industrial plants, and most forms of transportation

Lesson Activities

Environmental Concerns

1. Pollution is the dirtying of air, water, and land with chemicals and it is a side effect of living in an industrial society.
2. Pollution is a side effect of living in an industrial society
3. They fill up fast because we create so much garbage; they are undesirable and therefore hard to site; they can cause groundwater pollution.
4. Recycling means they will be reused, not added to a landfill or incinerated. This reduces pollution and conserves resources.
5. turn off lights; use less water; turn down the heat

Protecting the Air, Water, and Land

6. chemical waste from factories, landfills, pesticide runoff
7. the government required that lead be removed from gasoline
8. Radioactivity lasts a long time, some types remain harmful for thousands of years; pesticides can enter our water systems and are hard to get rid of.
9. radioactive waste, pesticides, batteries, motor oil, house paint, auto engine coolant
10. dumping toxic waste into the ocean won't get ride of the toxic waste, it will just sit there and leak into the ocean, our biggest and most vital body of water
11. Individuals have formed citizen groups to protect the environment and conserve natural resources. They work with local governments and businesses.
12. Clean Water Act, Clean Air Act, Endangered Species Act
13. *Local*: build mass transit systems; ban smoking in public places; work toward sustainable development *State*: inspect factories; enforce laws; ban smoking *Federal*: pass and enforce environmental laws

Check for Understanding

1-2. Local: build mass transit systems; ban smoking in public places; work toward sustainable development; State: inspect factories; enforce laws; ban smoking; Federal: pass and enforce environmental laws

3-4. Recycling reuses resources so more resources don't have to be used up, and keeps those products out of landfills

5-6. Landfills are filling up fast, so there is not a lot of free space to keep solid waste. The solid waste that is in a landfill is polluting water supplies, and no one wants to live near a landfill because it is unattractive and pollutes the area, so it is hard to find a place for one.

Citizens and the Law, Lesson 1

What Do You Know?

They allow people to live together in peace and help to prevent violence. Laws explain which actions are allowed in a society and which will be punished.

Answers will vary.

Lesson Activities

Why We Have Laws

1. Laws let everyone know which actions are permissible and discourage people from committing crimes.
2. Fair, reasonable, understandable, and enforceable. Students should underline, *A fair law treats people equally. Fair laws do not make different rules for different groups of people; To be reasonable, a law must not be too harsh. Cutting off someone's hand for stealing a loaf of bread would not be reasonable; They must be easy to understand. Otherwise people might break them without realizing it; Laws that are hard for police and other officials to enforce are not good laws.*

Development of the Legal System

3. about 3,800 years ago
4. As the Roman Empire grew, its laws and ideas were spread because the empire stretched over many regions.
5. the Justinian Code of the Byzantine Empire
6. Common law: law based on court decisions and customs instead of legal code, a combination of Roman law and canon law; Precedents: rulings made earlier in similar cases that judges would follow; Statutes: laws made by the legislature which contributed to the common law
7. A precedent is a legal decision based on a previous case made by a judge, a statute is a law made by a legislature.
8. Roman laws were simplified by a ruler named Justinian I into the Justinian Code. A long time later, French emperor Napoleon Bonaparte updated the Justinian Code into a new set of laws called the Napoleonic Code.

Types of Laws

9. public laws, criminal laws, civil laws
10. Criminal laws seek to protect public safety.
11. a felony
12. Property crimes are the most common; some examples are shoplifting, identity theft, and setting a fire.
13. court-martial
14. administrative law
15. the Constitution
16. case law
17. *Past*: Even prehistoric people had laws, or rules, outlining what people could and could not do; earliest laws were verbal; Babylonia is home to the oldest known written law, Code of Hammurabi; ancient Hebrews had laws outlined in the Ten Commandments; Justinian's Code, Roman law; Napoleonic Code, updated Roman code in 1804; English common law was brought to North America by early settlers. *Both*: laws were/are guides, rules; some past laws are still used today—do not kill, do not steal; If laws were/are broken, there is punishment for the offense. *Present*: There are three basic types of laws—criminal laws, civil laws, public laws; constitutional law deals with forming and interpreting constitutions; case law is based on judges' decisions; administrative law, executive branch doing its job; military law

Check for Understanding

1-2. to set which actions are allowed in society and which are not, set rules for working out problems over money, property and contracts, to help keep the peace

3. The colonists brought the traditions of common law and individual rights to North America when they settled. Both principles became key parts of U.S. laws.

4. constitutional law

Citizens and the Law, Lesson 2

What Do You Know?

The Constitution protects the people's rights by including protections that keep the government from using the law unfairly.

Lesson Activities

Basic Legal Rights

1. by banning authorities from punishing a person without a fair trial and for actions that were not illegal at the time, and by granting the right to have a judge review whether a person was rightfully imprisoned
2. Students should circle "A **bill of attainder** is a law that punishes a person without a trial. An **ex post facto law** punishes a person for doing something that was not illegal at the time it was done."
3. The due process clause in the Fourteenth Amendment strengthened a person's right to due process.

The Rights of the Accused

4. the Sixth Amendment; Article I
5. because it would breach the defendant's Fourth Amendment right to be protected from unreasonable searches and seizures
6. This right says that the federal government cannot deprive a person of life, liberty, or property without following the law.
7. Answers will vary, but it protects an accused person's rights by allowing him or her not to self-incriminate.
8. Students should underline the sentence that reads: "A grand jury is a group of people who decides whether the government has enough evidence to hold a trial."
9. The Sixth Amendment promises the accused that they have a right to know the charges against them, can question their accusers, have the right to be tried by an impartial jury, and have the right to legal representation.
10. This guarantee means that a punishment should fit the crime. It should not be overly harsh or overly lenient. For example, a life sentence for shoplifting would be too harsh; a fine for murder would be too lenient.
11. *Articles*: Article I of the Constitution, a person arrested has right to ask for writ of habeas corpus; Article I also forbids bills of attainder and ex post facto laws. *Amendments*: 5th and 14th Amendments, right of due process; 14th Amendment, equal protection clause; 4th Amendment, search warrant needed before entering a person's home; 5th Amendment, rights of accused—right to a grand jury, no self-incrimination; no double jeopardy; 6th Amendment, defendant has right to legal representation; 6th Amendment, speedy trial; 8th Amendment, prohibits cruel and unusual punishment and regulates bail

Check for Understanding

1-5. The basic legal rights include a guarantee against bills of attainder and ex post facto laws, as well as right to seek a writ of habeas corpus, the right to due process, and the right to the equal protection of the laws.

Civil and Criminal Law, Lesson 1

What Do You Know?

You might sue someone if he or she causes you some injury or breaks a contract with you.

A lawsuit begins with a plaintiff and a defendant. The plaintiff's lawyer files a complaint with the court, then the court sends the defendant a summons. Both lawyers gather evidence about the dispute and then one side offers the other a settlement. If the two sides don't settle, they go to court.

Lesson Activities

Types of Civil Law

1. A contract is an agreement or set of promises between two or more parties to exchange something of value.
2. Answers will vary; some examples are: ordering food, sharing a secret, and so on
3. family law
4. tort; negligence
5. acting in a careless or reckless way
6. contracts, property law, family law, personal injury or torts
7. People bring lawsuits to settle disputes that arise over contracts, property, family issues, personal injuries, and other matters of civil law.

The Legal Process in Civil Cases

8. First the complaint is filed by the plaintiff's lawyer, then the court sends a summons to the defendant. Both sides gather evidence about the dispute and then one side may offer a settlement. If both sides agree with the settlement they do not go to court.
9. the pre-trial stage when both sides in a lawsuit check facts and gather evidence

10. Damages and possibly punitive damages are awarded. Sometimes damages aren't awarded. The judge may order the defendant to take a certain action. The defendant may appeal the ruling to a higher court.
11. Damages are the money a court orders to be paid to a plaintiff for injuries or losses suffered.
12. Steps should include complaint, summons, discovery, trial, and appeal.
13. *Civil Law*: disputes between people; disputes between people and the government; cases are called lawsuits; four main types of civil law – contract law, property law, family law, personal injury, or torts; a tort is a wrongful act that causes injury; tort may be intentional or unintentional; lawsuits – plaintiff and defendant

Check for Understanding

1-2. intentional and negligent

3. A complaint is filed by the plaintiff's lawyer and states the wrong the defendant is accused of. A summons is the document that tells the defendant that he or she is being sued.

Civil and Criminal Law, Lesson 2

What Do You Know?

Criminal law is the type of law that deals with any act that breaks the law and harms people or society.

Lesson Activities

Crime and Punishment

1. A penal code is a document that lists crimes and their punishments.
2. a felony; even though the amount stolen was small, the threat of force against a person makes it a felony
3. Crimes can be classified either by the seriousness of the offense, such as misdemeanors and felonies, or by the nature of the offense, such as crimes against property and crimes against persons.
4. punishment; protecting society; warning to others; changing criminal behavior

Criminal Case Procedure

5. It starts and follows the legal process against a person who breaks the law.
6. booking, arraignment, trial, sentencing
7. arrest, booking, entering a plea (if crime is a misdemeanor)
8. They have to advise the suspect of the right to remain silent and the right to an attorney.
9. The prosecution presents evidence and the judge decides if there should be a trial.
10. The defendant either pleads guilty to the original crime or to a lesser crime in a plea bargain.
11. A lawyer for one side questions the other side's witnesses.
12. There are a range of penalties for crimes and each case is different. To be fair, a judge should have as much information as possible.
13. *Guilty*: if the suspect enters a guilty plea, plea bargaining begins; prosecution and defense try to reach a compromise; if they do, the case will never go to trial; if a case goes to trial and the defendant is found guilty, sentencing takes place at a later date; if the defendant is found guilty of a felony, they will often appeal the verdict to a higher court *Not guilty*: if the suspect enters a not guilty plea, the case goes to trial; defendants can choose to be tried by a jury or a judge; if jury, lawyers choose the jury from a group of people called for jury duty; defendants who are found to be not guilty are acquitted, or set free

Check for Understanding

1-2. an example of a misdemeanor would be stealing a $50 shirt from a store; an example of a felony would be using a gun to steal a $50 shirt from a store

3-4. Jury members must believe the accused is guilty beyond a reasonable doubt and, in most states, they must all agree.

Civil and Criminal Law, Lesson 3

What Do You Know?

Yes, youths are tried by a different system than adults. Youth are rehabilitated instead of punished.

When a youth breaks the law, he or she is taken into custody and may receive a warning or be turned over to the juvenile court if the offense is serious. A social worker then reviews the case and decides how it should be handled, and some cases are dismissed while others are sent to adult court. If the youth is still there after the reviewing, he or she goes to a detention hearing, then if charged an adjudication hearing, and if found delinquent to a disposition hearing.

From there the youth is sent to an institution or put on probation.

Lesson Activities

Juvenile Justice

1. Students should underline, "People began to believe that juveniles committed crimes because their families did not teach them proper values."
2. Juveniles have the right to know the charges against them, the right to an attorney, the right to cross-examine witnesses against them, and the right to remain silent.
3. *Delinquent offenders*: have committed acts that would be crimes if committed by adults; have same legal rights as adults; in many states a juvenile charged with a felony can be tried as an adult *Status offenders*: have committed acts that would not be crimes if committed by adults; examples include – skipping school, running away from home, staying out after curfew; status offenders are usually put under court supervision; parents or guardians are unable to supervise the offender

The Juvenile Court System

4. A juvenile court can remove these children from their homes. The court places them with other families.
5. to take charge or control of someone in an official way
6. starting from top left and moving down: custody; intake; the state makes the case that the youth should be charged; adjudication hearing; the judge sentences the delinquent offender
7. A social worker reviews the case and decides how to proceed. Not all cases remain in juvenile court.
8. diversion
9. An adjudication hearing is like a trial; a disposition hearing is like a sentencing hearing.
10. *Neglect Cases*: young people suffer abuse or neglect from parents or guardians; *Both*: juvenile courts handle both types of cases; children can be removed from their parents or guardians; *Delinquency Cases*: young people break the law; they are taken into custody; the case can be turned over to juvenile court if it is serious; some cases are dismissed, some cases go to adult court, sometimes the juvenile is sent for counseling or drug treatment

Check for Understanding

1. Before the mid-1800s youths were tried and sentenced like adults. Today youths are not treated as adults unless the crime is serious. They are rehabilitated and punishments are less severe.

2-3. neglect and delinquency cases

Introduction to Economics, Lesson 1

What Do You Know?

People have to make choices between wants when there are few resources.

Economic choices are decisions on how limited resources should be used. Economic choices are decided by the questions *what goods and services will be produced, how will the goods and services be produced, who will consume the goods and services*?

Lesson Activities

Our Wants and Resources

1. Wants are things people would like to have.
2. Natural resources: flour, cheese, tomatoes; Labor: pizza makers and delivery people; Capital: store building, pizza ovens
3. Economics is the study of how people and groups deal with the problem of scarcity.
4. Scarcity, or not having enough resources, to produce all the things that would satisfy all wants, is the basic economic problem faced by both people and nations.

Societies and Economic Choices

5. *Limited*: Resources are limited; there aren't enough resources to satisfy everyone's wants and needs; scarcity occurs when resources are limited; no country has all the resources it needs *Unlimited*: Wants are unlimited; individuals, cities, states, and national governments have wants and needs
6. its answers to the three basic economic questions
7. its resources
8. Student should underline: way of producing the things people want and need
9. a command economy
10. *Traditional*: People own their resources and base their economic choices on habits or customs. *Market*: Resources are owned by an individual or a business. They make their decisions based on prices. *Command*: The government owns the resources and decides which goods to produce. *Mixed Market*:

Businesses and people produce the goods and the government makes rules for those businesses to follow.

Check for Understanding

1. Scarcity forces people and governments to make economic choices.
2. Societies must decide what to produce, how to produce it, and who will get the products. By choosing an economic system, a society decides how it will answer these questions.

Introduction to Economics, Lesson 2

What Do You Know?

A trade-off is giving up one option in order to get something of greater value.

Lesson Activities

Trade-Offs

1. It is the alternative that the decision maker must trade off, or give up, for a more desirable option.
2. When times are hard, taxes go down and governments do not have as much money to spend. They have to make choices that involve trade-offs.

Measuring Costs and Revenues

3. It says that you made the wrong choice.
4. the money a producer receives from selling a good or service
5. Longer hours for workers equals more costs in wages. Selling more food means buying more ingredients.
6. $30, no
7. $30
8. Students should circle "marginal revenues" and "marginal costs" in the text.
9. the additional benefit with the additional cost; if the benefit is greater than the cost, then the project or action is worth doing
10. marginal revenue and marginal cost; when the two lines cross, the marginal revenue is the same as the marginal cost
11. *Fixed Costs*: expenses that stay the same no matter how much a business produces; *Variable Costs*: expenses that change when a business produces more or less; *Total Cost*: a business' fixed costs and variable costs combined; *Marginal Cost*: how much expenses go up if more is produced

Check for Understanding

1. A trade-off is a kind of economic choice. The opportunity cost is what you give up when you make a trade-off.
2. It can help a business decide whether it will gain revenue by expanding and exactly how much.

Introduction to Economics, Lesson 3

What Do You Know?

Producers are the people and businesses that provide goods and services that create supply, and consumers are the people who buy goods and services that create demand. Supply is the amount of a good or service that producers are willing and able to sell at various prices during a set time period, while demand is the amount of good or service that people are willing and able to buy at a particular price, so supply and demand rely on each other.

Lesson Activities

Demand and Supply Make Markets

1. demand and supply
2. When prices go up, supply goes up. When prices go down, supply goes down.
3. demand falls; as prices increase, supply also increases
4. the lower the price per barrel, the higher quantity demanded
5. Increased competition keeps prices down to attract buyers, because if the competition is offering lower prices, buyers will go there instead.
6. $30 a barrel
7. A surplus occurs when supply is greater than demand. A shortage occurs when demand is greater than supply.
8. the number of consumers and consumer income
9. increase in the number of consumers, increase in consumers' income, increase in consumers' likes (preferences)
10. They are produced for those who have the desire and money to buy them at a set price.
11. Student answers will vary but should show an understanding of what affects supply and demand, based on the table.

The Economic Role of Prices

12. in a market economy; because prices are the result of the interaction of supply and

demand, whereas in a command economy they are fixed by the government

13. *Demand*: how much of a good or service people are willing or able to buy; *Both*: prices and demand are connected because the cost of goods determines demand, and demand changes as prices change; *Prices*: how much something costs; they determine what to produce, who products are produced for, how they are produced

Check for Understanding

1. Demand falls as prices rise.
2. Prices can act as a signal for consumer demand. This leads businesses to adjust prices or stop producing items that consumers do not want.

The American Economy, Lesson 1

What Do You Know?

the total market value of all final goods and services produced in one year

Society has to think about resources, what they will receive for the money, who will be affected, and if it is necessary.

Lesson Activities

Why GDP Is Important

1. taking a guitar lesson, being served food at a restaurant
2. sneakers, clothing, sports equipment
3. *Entrepreneur*: a person who takes a risk to start a new business; an entrepreneur is a factor of production; businesses bring the three factors of production together—land, labor, capital
4. labor and entrepreneur
5. GDP represents income for all factors of production because these factors are used in producing products, and companies must pay workers and owners of the other factors for their use.

Measuring GDP

6. Reselling a good does not involve new production, and they were counted when they were originally sold.
7. final goods: a sweater, a greeting card; intermediate goods: colored ink, thread
8. the price of final goods and services, and how many were sold
9. GDP is the total dollar value of all final goods and services produced in a country during a single year; GDP per capita is that amount divided by the number of people, or the amount of GDP per person
10. 2000
11. The standard of living for a country with a high GDP per capita would be higher than the standard of living for a country with a low GDP per capita.
12. *Definition*: GDP is the value of all the final products made in a country in one year. GDP tells how large a country's economy is. *Represents*: the income of the people who make goods and provide services; making goods and providing services is called labor

Check for Understanding

1. it shows the income and standard of living of a country
2. the hope that the business will be profitable
3. GDP measures the size of a country's economy.

The American Economy, Lesson 2

What Do You Know?

Resources, goods, and services all make the economy run.

An economy grows when a population grows or becomes more productive.

Lesson Activities

The Circular Flow Model

1. capital, labor, natural resources, entrepreneurs
2. product markets, business sector, factor markets, consumer sector
3. the factor market
4. consumers
5. Students should underline, "The consumer sector is made up of all the people who get paid and buy goods and services."
6. Students should underline "money always flows in a clockwise direction" in the lesson's sixth paragraph
7. Answers will vary, but should demonstrate an understanding of the concept of the product market. Students may mention buying something at a product market such as a supermarket, a store in a mall, or a Web site.

Promoting Economic Growth

8. The government sector is made up of federal, state, and local governments that buy products and services in the product market and sell goods and services to earn

income. The Foreign sector is made up of the people and businesses from other countries that buy and sell goods in the United States.

9. Economic growth raises people's standard of living.
10. The GDP is the total dollar value of all the final goods and services of a country in a year. The GDP per capita is the GDP per person, or the GDP divided by population.
11. when a large job is broken down into smaller tasks, productivity increases
12. *Productivity Improves*: Economic growth occurs when resources are used efficiently.; *Business Improves*: Businesses can improve by specializing in one product or service, which helps productivity.; Specialization allows businesses and employees to become specialists, or experts.; *Workers Improve*: Division of labor, or dividing work into smaller tasks, allows workers to do their job faster and better. Workers gain training, education, and experience.

Check for Understanding

1-2. product market, factor market

3-5. raise productivity, specialize in a product, focus on human capital

The American Economy, Lesson 3

What Do You Know?

Capitalism is an economic system in which private citizens own the factors of production and decide how to use them to make money.

Lesson Activities

Capitalism in the United States

1. Student should circle, "free enterprise."
2. The market is the place where buyers and sellers interact. Consumers demand products and services, and businesses supply them. Voluntary exchange is when buyers and sellers choose to take part in an exchange. The profit motive is the desire to make money that encourages a person to offer a product to buyers. Competition is when businesses that sell similar products try to attract customers; Private property owners
3. Property rights create an incentive for people to invest in and take care of their property.
4. Entrepreneurs take a risk to start a business and work for themselves. Laborers work for entrepreneurs or other businesses, not for themselves.
5. Student should underline, "The second feature is the market. The market is the place where buyers and sellers interact. Supply and demand drive the U.S. markets. Consumers like you demand products and services. Businesses supply them."
6. Voluntary means choosing to take part in something.
7. economic freedom, the market, voluntary exchange, the profit motive, competition, private property rights
8. the profit motive, or the wish to earn money

The Origins of U.S. Capitalism

9. The nation's founders were influenced by Smith's ideas and thus created a government that reflected those ideas.
10. Adam Smith believed that markets worked best without government interference.
11. Student answers will vary and might include: citizens make most of the economic decisions; Adam Smith; The Wealth of Nations; laissez-faire economics; competition is allowed; government should stay out of the marketplace; private citizens own the factors of production; free enterprise; businesses can compete with each other

Check for Understanding

1-2. Private property rights give people the incentive to work, save, and invest and motivate people to take care their property.

3-4. government should not interfere with the marketplace; government should act only to ensure competition is free

Personal Finance, Lesson 1

What Do You Know?

Consumer rights are the rights people have when they buy things such as product safety and reliability.

Consumers must distinguish between what they want and what they need and figure out how much money they have to spend.

Lesson Activities

Consumer Rights

1. a person who buys goods and services
2. The FDA guarantees the safety of food, drugs, and medicine, while the FTC protects consumers from businesses that are dishonest and act unfairly
3. redress

4. the right to safe products; the right to accurate information; the right to choose among competing products; the right to be heard; the right to redress; the right to environmental health; the right to service; the right to consumer education

Consumer Responsibilities

5. Consumer rights are rights given to consumers to protect them, while consumer responsibilities are responsibilities the consumer must uphold in order to ensure making smart shopping decisions, like gathering information on a product.
6. comparison shopping
7. Students should underline "One responsibility is to make smart decisions about what you buy", in the first paragraph; "Another responsibility is to report any problems with a product", in the fourth paragraph; and "That means consumers also have a responsibility to be honest with producers and sellers. A consumer should not try to return a product to the store if he or she broke it", in the last paragraph.
8. research a product, analyze ads, comparison shop

Making Purchasing Decisions

9. disposable income
10. Answers will vary but should show an understanding of disposable and discretionary income.
11. Answers should show an understanding of opportunity cost.
12. *Rights*: consumer safety; a variety of goods and services should be available to consumers at competitive prices; products and services should be presented honestly; 1906, FDA (Food and Drug Administration); FTC (Federal Trade Commission); consumer bill of rights; *Responsibilities*: comparison shopping; make smart decisions on what products to buy; practice consumerism

Check for Understanding

1-2. different stores, online options, generic products

3-4. learn to distinguish between needs and wants and how to balance the two; avoid impulse buying; calculate the opportunity cost of an item before buying

Personal Finance, Lesson 2

What Do You Know?

Income, expenses, balance

Credit is money borrowed to pay for goods or services. Credit lets you buy now and pay later.

Lesson Activities

Using a Personal Budget

1. *Expenses*: the money spent for wants and needs; if expenses are less than income, there is not a deficit; *Balance*: the money left after expenses have been paid; if there is more income than expenses, there is a surplus; *Surplus*: a surplus exists if there is more income than expenses; *Deficit*: a deficit exists if there are more expenses than income
2. Income – Expenses = Balance
3. To make a budget, you should list your expenses and your income. Then calculate your balance. Use this information to decide whether you need to spend less money or make more money. Once the budget is made, use it to keep track of your spending.
4. One in which income matches expenses.

Using Credit

5. Student should underline, "Credit is money borrowed to pay for goods or services. Credit lets you buy now and pay later."
6. Borrowing money would mean that you had another expense (the loan payment) in your budget. You would need to make sure you had the necessary income to cover this new expense.
7. Anyone can use a bank, but credit unions can only be used by their members.
8. Students should underline, "To be approved for credit, you have to have a history of paying back the money you borrowed in the past."
9. a payment for part of the purchase price; often used for homes, cars
10. credit cards
11. borrowing more than you can afford and getting into financial trouble
12. You might over-borrow and overspend and be unable to make your payments, placing yourself in financial difficulty.
13. *Loans*: A loan is money that a person borrows for a fee and often requires a down payment on what you are purchasing. Loans allow you to borrow large amounts of money to use for big things like houses and cars. *Credit Cards*: The most common form of credit is credit cards, which can be issued by banks, credit card companies, or stores. Credit cards have a limit on how much you can borrow. They are generally used for small items.

Check for Understanding

1-2. banks, stores, credit unions

3-4. What is the APR? How long do I have to make the payments? What are the penalties for late payments? Are there extra fees?

Personal Finance, Lesson 3

What Do You Know?

Saving some of your income means there is emergency money and money saved up for big purchases.

Saving plans are ways to save up money through savings accounts, money market accounts, or certificates of deposit.

Stocks and bonds have higher returns, so if you invest in them you may get more money back than other methods, but there is a risk of losing some or all of your money.

Lesson Activities

Saving Money

1. Principal is the money that you have deposited into your savings account, while interest is the payment people receive when they let the bank use their money.
2. job loss, unexpected car repair, natural disaster, home repairs, unexpected medical bills
3. checks, debit cards, electronic banking
4. Students should underline the following words in the first paragraph: fees, charged, withdrawn at any time, and paying; Penalty is the fee for early withdrawal of funds from a certificate of deposit.

Savings Plans

5. because access to your funds is restricted for a longer period of time; i.e., the bank is using your money for a longer period of time
6. a checking account

Stocks and Bonds

7. If a company goes out of business then all a stockholders money can be lost.
8. $1000; $1000
9. Selling a stock for higher than the original price results in a profit. A dividend is when the company pays the stockholder a portion of their profit.
10. by using a large pool of money to spread investments over a wide array of stocks and bonds.
11. *Saving Money*: setting money aside, in an accessible account, so it is available to use later; *Both*: Both saving and investing offer returns, or profit, but at differing rates. *Investing Money*: putting money into an account or buying a part of a company to get a return, or profit; Investing can be highly beneficial, but it can also be a risk.

Check for Understanding

1. Savings are important for helping a person reach long-term goals, in case of emergencies, and to help the economy.

2-3. savings accounts, money market accounts, and CDs

4. stocks, bonds, mutual funds

Business in America, Lesson 1

What Do You Know?

A sole proprietorship is a business owned by one person.

A partnership is a business owned by two or more people.

Lesson Activities

Sole Proprietorships

1. Student should underline, "a business owned by one person".
2. The owner or proprietor receives all the profits.

Partnerships

3. *General*: when all partners own the business; all partners share the profits and debts, and all run the business; *Limited*: has general partners as well as limited partners; partners give money towards the business and share in the profits but do not help run it
4. a business owned by two or more people; for example, starting a restaurant with a friend, where each puts in the same amount of money to start the restaurant and each has an equal say in how the business is run
5. The two types of partnerships are general partnerships and limited partnerships.

Corporations

6. It makes the owner personally responsible for the business's debts and legal judgments.
7. Students should underline "Shareholders (Stockholders)" and circle "Board of Directors."
8. The president is hired by the board of directors. The board is elected by the stockholders.

9. The employees are the ones that do all the work in the departments that make the corporation successful.
10. Student should underline, "easy to raise money"; "have a long life"; "limited liability"
11. The stockholders are the corporation's owners.
12. Student advertisements will vary but should illustrate the advantages of the form of business they have chosen.
13. A franchise owner buys the right to sell a product in a certain location.
14. lack of control over the business
15. It does not seek to make a profit.
16. The three forms of businesses are sole proprietorship, partnership, corporation. In a franchise the owner pays a fee and part of profits to a supplier. Businesses are for-profit, meaning they want to earn a profit. Some businesses are nonprofit organizations. A cooperative is a form of nonprofit business to help cooperative members.

Check for Understanding

1-3. sole proprietorship; partnership; corporation

4-6. own boss, unlimited liability; easier to raise money, unlimited liability; limited liability, increased government regulations

Business in America, Lesson 2

What Do You Know?

Negotiation through injunction, mediation, and arbitration

Lesson Activities

Organized Labor

1. improving wages and working conditions; regulating working hours; making sure equipment is safe
2. Union membership has decreased over the years as manufacturing jobs have gone down and service jobs gone up.
3. In a trade union all members work in the same trade or craft. An industrial union includes all workers in an industry, regardless of their job.
4. Because the laws give workers a choice of joining a union or not, they might lead to lower union membership. Employers can also discourage the organization of a union in their business. As a result people who might want to join a union may not have the option.
5. Recently labor unions have been in decline as right-to-work laws have been banning union shops and unions represent fewer workers overall than they used to.
6. a process in which labor and management meet to work out a contract

Labor Negotiations

7. A business cannot survive without its workers. The company will lose money for each day the employees do not work. Management will be forced to give in.
8. In a strike, workers voluntarily stop working; in a lockout, the employer prevents workers from entering the workplace and working.
9. ordered to end a strike; ordered to end a lockout; ask for an order to end a lockout that endangers national security
10. when the strike threatens the nation's welfare or security
11. injunction, mediation, arbitration
12. *Mediation*: Mediation depends on a third party making a compromise with the union and employer. *Arbitration*: Arbitration is when a third party makes the decision for the employer and union.

Check for Understanding

1. Both bring in a third party to help reach an agreement. In mediation the third party helps reach a compromise. In arbitration the third party decides on a solution.

Business in America, Lesson 3

What Do You Know?

Businesses supply the food, clothing, and shelter in communities, as well as giving away free products and donating money to causes. Some small businesses supply free services to the poor and nonprofit groups.

Businesses have the responsibility of making products that are safe for its consumers to buy and to have truthful advertising. Businesses have the responsibility of transparency to its owners as they have a right to know what's going on since they do not manage the company. Businesses are responsible for a safe workplace for their employees and fair treatment of their employees.

Lesson Activities

The Social Responsibility of Businesses

1. They do it to be socially responsible; to benefit society as well as themselves. They set up foundations, sponsor schools, or donate their time and skills.

2. an organization set up to give money to causes that promote the public good
3. Students should underline, "About 75% of small companies also give money to help others. Some professionals give free services to the poor or to nonprofit groups."
4. $14.1 billion; because foundations are set up by wealthy people or businesses to give money.
5. religion, education, foundations, human services, public-society benefit, health, international affairs, arts, culture and humanities, environment and animals, individuals

Other Business Responsibilities

6. crucial, reveal
7. so owners or potential stockholders can make informed decisions about whether to invest in the company
8. *Community*: local government supports businesses; community can refer people to local businesses; community members can buy locally; *Business*: must use honest advertising; provide safe goods and services to the community; may donate money or services to those in need or set up foundations to help people; should treat customers fairly

Check for Understanding

1-4. consumers, owners/stockholders, employees, communities

5. Answers will vary; Communities support their local businesses in a variety of ways. Companies have a responsibility to return the loyalty the communities show them.

Government's Role in the Economy, Lesson 1

What Do You Know?

Goods are things that can be used, either by an individual or by many individuals, and services are work provided either for free or for a price, like a haircut and public parks.

taking part in a competitive market, creating safe products

The government can protect consumers by keeping monopolies from forming; it has created agencies to oversee the safety of food, medical equipment, and other products.

Lesson Activities

Providing Public Goods

1. Student answers should fit the definition of private goods.
2. The government collects taxes and other fees to pay for public goods.
3. Most public goods come from the government because it can tax people and use that money for public goods, but it is hard for businesses to charge everyone who uses public goods.
4. a negative externality

Maintaining Competition

5. several businesses banded together that threaten competition
6. a monopoly; rents might be high because any person wishing to rent in that town would be forced to pay whatever price the owner demanded
7. The government may allow a monopoly if it benefits consumers by keeping prices low.
8. The government regulates competition to prevent businesses from controlling a market and raising prices.

Providing Consumer Health and Safety

9. The FDA oversees the safety of food, drugs, medical equipment, and cosmetics.
10. to ensure that the meat it produces is safe for public consumption
11. *handle competition*: prevents monopolies; passes antitrust laws to prevent trusts and keep competition in the marketplace; *provide public goods and services*: provides public goods that are used by many people such as sidewalks, parks, roads, public libraries, government buildings; public services include police protection, fire protection, and national defense; *regulate business*: besides encouraging competition, the government also regulates other business activities such as natural monopolies, product advertising, and product safety.

Check for Understanding

1. The government is mostly involved in providing public goods. It takes on this responsibility because businesses do not want to do so.
2. The major laws are the Sherman Antitrust Act of 1890 and the Clayton Antitrust Act of 1914. The overriding goal of these laws is to encourage fair competition in the marketplace.

Government's Role in the Economy, Lesson 2

What Do You Know?

A nation's economy is important because many parts of people's daily lives depend on a healthy economy that can meet their needs and wants.

The stock market is a market where stocks, or shares of ownership in businesses, are bought and sold.

Lesson Activities

Economic Performance

1. Answers will vary, may include a playground seesaw or a roller coaster at an amusement park.
2. recession
3. Students should underline, "The economy does not grow at a steady rate. Instead it goes through ups and downs. This series of ups and downs is called the **business cycle.**"
4. A peak on a business cycle graph is the highest point of growth preceding a decline.
5. *expansion*: periods of growth and expansion are longer than periods of decline; most last from 6 to 10 years; *recession*: if real GDP is low for six months or more the economy is in a recession; usually last less than a year; longest recession since 1930s was from December 2007 to June 2008; *depression*: period of severe economic decline; recession can turn into a depression if real GDP continues to go down instead of turning back up; Great Depression started with stock market crash in 1929.
6. Answers will vary but should include an understanding that a depression is more severe than a recession, but both involve a sustained drop in real GDP.

Other Measures of Performance

7. Students should underline the following sentences in paragraphs 1 and 2: "The unemployment rate is the number of civilians who are out of work and looking for a job." "The civilian labor force is made up of all of the people 16 and older who are either working or are looking for work."
8. If the unemployment rate is going up, the economy is doing poorly. Unemployment ususally goes up during recessions, when GDP is going down.
9. Inflation reduces purchasing power because rising prices mean that a given amount of money can buy less than before.

Economic Indicators

10. bull market
11. The Leading Economic Index combines ten sets of data to try to predict economic activity in the future.
12. *real GDP*: measure of Gross Domestic Product after adjustments have been made for inflation or higher prices; gives a better picture of an economy over time than GDP; *unemployment*: the number of people in the civilian labor force who are out of work and looking for jobs; high unemployment means the economy is troubled.; *prices*: if prices remain constant then people and businesses can plan and budget better; when prices go up, money loses its value; when prices go up for a long time it is called inflation; *stock market*: the overall performance of the stock market is an economic indicator; Dow-Jones Industrial Average (DJIA) and Standard and Poor's (S&P) are the most common stock indexes; a falling market is called a bear market; a rising stock market is called a bull market; bull markets are a sign that the economy is doing well.

Check for Understanding

1. Business leaders want to be able to plan for the future. Government leaders want to know if their policies are working.
2. When stock prices rise overall, it is a sign that the economy is doing well. When stock prices fall overall, this can signal problems in the economy and possibly even a coming recession.

Government's Role in the Economy, Lesson 3

What Do You Know?

stay in school and pursue further degrees

The government gives out welfare, which pays for many necessities, and often people receive unemployment insurance.

Lesson Activities

Income Inequality

1. Students should underline education, family wealth, and discrimination.
2. Dropouts earn lower wages and face higher rates of unemployment.
3. education, family wealth, and discrimination
4. Higher education levels lead to higher income levels on average.
5. It allows for more people to enter the job market and fill higher paying jobs they are

qualified for. This could lead to higher economic growth.

6. It bans discrimination on the basis of gender, race, color, religion, and national origin; 1964
7. It allows women who have experienced gender discrimination in the workplace to sue their employers.

Poverty

8. Welfare is money or necessities given to the poor. Examples include TANF, unemployment compensation, and workers' compensation.
9. Poverty guidelines reflect the amount of money one needs in order to be able to afford the basic necessities to survive. These guidelines determine whether someone is able to receive benefits from certain welfare programs.
10. people who have lost their jobs and are looking for work
11. Economic Opportunities: government gives money to programs that help students stay in school and graduate; government loans and grants are offered to help students attend college; laws have been passed to help prevent discrimination such as Fair Pay Act, Civil Rights Act, Equal Employment Opportunity Act; Both: government tries to help those who don't have economic stability; government needs revenue for programs; Poverty Aid: the government provides welfare—money or necessities given to the poor; Temporary Assistance to Needy Families (TANF); unemployment insurance provides compensation for workers who lose their jobs; workers compensations helps workers harmed on the job

Check for Understanding

1. Government programs help people go to college. Federal laws protect people from discrimination, which also affects income.
2. through programs such as Temporary Assistance for Needy Families, by setting a minimum wage, and by providing unemployment and workers' compensation

The Government and Banking, Lesson 1

What Do You Know?

The value of money comes from the measure of value that is put on it by others and the fact that it is an agreed-upon medium of exchange.

businesses that store money for and loan money to other businesses and individuals

Lesson Activities

All About Money

1. medium of exchange, store of value, and measure of value
2. chocolate coins are not very durable
3. Medium of Exchange: money is a medium, or means, of exchange; it is a way to exchange goods and services; people barter, or trade, if they don't have money; Store of Value: money is a store of value; it is a way to hold wealth; it can be kept until it is needed for use; Measure of Value: how much money something costs can be used to determine its value
4. electronic money
5. electronic money, coins, paper money
6. Watermarks and security threads make official currency difficult to duplicate, which limits the supply. If it was easy to duplicate, everyone would make currency and it would lose its worth.
7. Student answers will vary.

Financial Institutions

8. deposits
9. Banks take deposits made by customers and lend that money to other businesses and individuals. Banks charge interest and fees on these loans to make money.
10. businesses that store money for and loan money to other businesses and individuals
11. commercial banks, credit unions, and savings and loan associations
12. Commercial banks provide full banking services to people and businesses. S&Ls work like commercial banks but the biggest difference is that most of their customers are individuals rather than businesses.
13. Student rewrites will vary but should show an understanding of credit unions.
14. a government-run deposit insurance program that backs bank deposits up to $250,000
15. to make banks safe; this makes people trust the banking system, which allows the economy to grow
16. *Financial Institutions*: commercial banks, S&Ls, credit unions; *Types of Money*: Currency is paper money, coins, electronic money

Check for Understanding

1. Yes. Electronic money has unlimited portability. It is divisible into any size. It is durable, as long as the computer files are not tampered with. It is in limited supply because

only people who have the appropriate information can access the money.

2-4. take deposits, offer checking and savings accounts, make loans

The Government and Banking, Lesson 2

What Do You Know?

the central bank of the government

manages money, watches over commercial banks, and helps keep the U.S. economy healthy

Lesson Activities

The Fed's Structure

1. so that banks would have a place from which to borrow money during economic hard times
2. manages money, watches over commercial banks, and helps keep the U.S. economy healthy
3. the Federal Reserve System
4. About 2,900 commercial banks
5. There are 12 Federal Reserve Banks with 25 branches.
6. to manage the country's money supply

What the Fed Does

7. The Fed regulates monetary policy to keep prices stable and help the economy grow at an even rate.
8. it pushes interest rates down; arrow should point down, it pushes interest rates up; arrow should point up
9. It grows the money supply because this causes interest rates to go down, which encourages borrowing.
10. open market operations, the discount rate, the reserve requirement
11. Student answers will vary but should show an understanding of the discount rate.
12. The Fed can keep check of how much lending banks do by increasing or decreasing the reserve requirement.
13. *Increasing Reserve*: When the money supply is decreased, interest rates go up and people borrow less money. *Decreasing Reserve*: When the money supply is increased, interest rates go down, which encourages people to borrow money.

Check for Understanding

1-2. The Fed conducts monetary policy, regulates banks, takes care of the currency, and acts as the government's bank.

3. Increasing the reserve requirement decreases the money supply because banks have less money to loan. Decreasing the reserve requirement increases the money supply because banks have more money to loan.

The Government and Banking, Lesson 3

What Do You Know?

savings accounts, certificates of deposit, checking accounts, and money market accounts

the national government

Lesson Activities

Banks in the Economy

1. savings account, certificate of deposit
2. Underline: pay more interest, Circle: fixed term; lower interest rate as a penalty
3. savings accounts are used to save money and make it grow; checking accounts are used to pay expenses
4. A bank loan is money borrowed from a bank by a person or a business. Loan terms are the purpose, amount borrowed, interest rate, and length of the loan.

How Banking Has Changed

5. some leaders feared it would become too powerful
6. During this time the Second Bank of the United States was created and many state banks also sprang up. These banks were not regulated. As a result the banking system became more and more chaotic.
7. The states did not have enough control of the banks. Banks were making their own paper money. The banks printed too many notes and caused inflation.
8. There was a lack of cooperation between the 12 bank districts, which made it difficult for the Federal Reserve to stop the Great Depression.
9. This law protects deposits and has given the Federal Reserve more power to keep the economy under control.
10. 1929; the Great Depression
11. Putting S&Ls under the FDIC program and increasing oversight made them safer.
12. because banks had been making risky loans, they had no money
13. *Banks Succeed*: people and businesses store money in banks; people feel their deposits and accounts are safe; banks lend money to individuals and businesses; some

borrowers invest money back into the community; banks pay interest on deposits; *Banks Fail*: people panic and distrust the banks; the government, through the FDIC, backs every bank with deposit insurance in case the bank goes out of business; up to $250,000 is protected for each customer

Check for Understanding

1. Banks provide financial services, including offering various types of accounts and making loans.

2-3. creation of Federal Reserve System, Banking Act of 1933

Financing the Government, Lesson 1

What Do You Know?

The government uses its revenues, which mainly come from personal income taxes and other taxes, to pay for services.

Lesson Activities

Understanding the Federal Budget

1. spend less money or make more money

2. Both involve weighing income and expenditures and making choices, but the federal budget is more time-consuming with more people involved.

3. *Revenue*: Revenue is how much money the federal government has available to spend. Personal income tax, paid on money earned, is the largest source of revenue for the federal government. Payroll taxes and corporate income taxes are two other sources of revenue; *Expenditures*: The federal government uses revenue to pay expenses. The government's two biggest expenditures are national defense and social security.

4. Mandatory spending is written into law and doesn't need approval every year. Discretionary spending is a choice that is made and approved every year.

5. income and payroll taxes; Social Security and defense

6. The federal government spent 13% of its budget on Medicare.

Budgeting for State and Local Governments

7. States are required by law to balance their budgets. They cannot borrow money to make up for too little revenue, as the federal government can.

8. money that one level of government gets from another

9. debt; education

10. education, police and fire protection, libraries, water service, sewage, trash collection, and street repair

11. *Federal*: from personal income, payroll, and corporate income taxes; *State*: from the federal government and state sales taxes; some states have income taxes; *Local*: from their state government, local sales taxes, property taxes, traffic fines and other fees

Check for Understanding

1-2. state government, the federal government

3. State governments have to pay for services such as police and firefighters. The federal government can borrow money, state governments cannot.

Financing the Government, Lesson 2

What Do You Know?

When there is a budget surplus, the government saves that money to balance the budget when revenues are low, and when there is a budget deficit the government borrows money to balance it.

Lesson Activities

Surpluses and Deficits

1. budgets are based on predictions and predictions can be wrong

2. They are opposites. A surplus is when revenues exceed spending; a deficit is when spending exceeds revenues.

3. The federal government keeps spending more money than it collects. It must borrow money to make up the difference.

4. It has mostly run a budget deficit over the last two decades.

5. 2000

6. higher interest payments; slowing economy; loss of confidence

Managing the Economy

7. to keep unemployment low; to help the economy grow; to make goods and services available

8. the government's use of taxes and spending to influence the economy

9. The government uses fiscal policy during an economic slowdown to try to stimulate the economy and make it grow again.

10. it is hard to agree on; it is slow; its effects are unpredictable

11. Students should underline, "These programs help the economy automatically, without other action from the government."
12. They start working automatically to counter the effects of a recession.
13. *Budget Surplus*: a surplus occurs when more money is collected than is spent; it can be used for emergencies or to supplement times when there is a deficit; *Budget Deficit*: a deficit occurs when more money is spent than is collected; 49 of the 50 states have laws that say they must have a balanced budget; States cannot borrow money. They have to cut spending, raise taxes, or both.

Check for Understanding

1. A government may have to sell bonds, cut programs, or increase taxes to make up for the deficit.

2-3. federal borrowing can cause higher interest rates; investors can lose confidence in the government; interest on the debt is costly; federal borrowing slows the economy

International Trade and Economic Systems, Lesson 1

What Do You Know?

Nations do not always have the resources they need to make the things their people want.

Lesson Activities

Trade Between Nations

1. imports: goods produced in other nations that are brought into the country, exports: goods a country produces that it sells to other nations
2. the cost of the next best use of time or money when choosing to do one thing or another
3. China: producing goods that require lots of labor; Brazil: producing crops
4. China's population is large. That gives it a big work force. Most people are paid low wages, so the price of Chinese labor is lower. That is why China makes products that require a lot of labor to produce.
5. *Tariff*: a tax on imports; a tariff raises the price of imported goods; Governments might place tariffs on imported goods to protect local producers and their market. *Quota*: A quota limits the amount of an item that can come into a country. Placing quotas allows prices to stay high for locally produced goods.
6. Nations sometimes impose tariffs to raise prices of imported goods and make domestic goods more competitive.
7. Quotas keep prices higher. Arrow should point up.
8. Trade barriers are set up to protect industries at home from foreign competition. Free trade is meant to increase trade by lowering trade barriers.
9. Student's should underline, "The World Trade Organization (WTO) helps regulate international trade."

Balance of Trade

10. balance of trade; trade deficit–importing more than exporting
11. Trade barriers set up by other countries might help lead to a trade deficit at home. The barriers would reduce the amount of goods the nation could sell abroad, thus reducing the value of its exports overall.
12. The exchange rate is the value of one nation's currency in relation to another's.
13. Heavy imports can lead to the dollar being more available in markets where currency is sold, which drives down the price. This can be good for exports, as goods will be cheaper for other countries.
14. *Trade Surplus*: occurs when a nation exports more than it imports; leads to a strong economy *Trade Deficit*: occurs when a nation imports more than it exports; trade deficits can slow down an economy; jobs can be lost; value of currency can drop

Check for Understanding

1-2. One is that it cannot produce some goods that people need and want. The second reason is that other nations have a comparative advantage in the production of certain goods.

3. A trade surplus occurs when the value of a nation's exports is greater than the value of its imports. It means the country does not need to borrow money from other nations to pay for imported goods.

International Trade and Economic Systems, Lesson 2

What Do You Know?

people make economic decisions, prices are determined by supply and demand, there is individual freedom

Mixed economies combine parts of a market economy and a centrally-planned economy, which might be better for some countries since the market and the government are both important in this type of economy.

Lesson Activities

Market Economies

1. In a market economy, individuals own the factors of production.
2. The GDP is the total value of goods produced in a nation, the GDP per capita is total value of goods produced by a country divided by its population.
3. people own the factors of production, high GDP; profit-driven so it is possible to have poor wages, do not grow at a steady rate
4. people own factors of production and make own economic choices; they do not grow steadily, can result in negative externalities

Command Economies

5. In a command economy, the government controls the economic decisions and factors of production.
6. Supply does not depend on demand in a command economy, but rather on the decisions of central planners. Because of this, shortages of consumer goods can occur.
7. Privatization is the change from having state-owned businesses and farms to ones owned by private citizens.
8. Students should underline "GDP and GDP per capita have grown," "pollution," and "growing gap between income groups."

Mixed Economies

9. free markets and government control
10. Signs that the United States does not have a pure market economy are the fact that the government provides some goods and services, sets rules to make markets competitive, and regulates some businesses.

Developed and Developing Countries

11. developed countries have a high standard of living and a lot of industry; developing countries are not very productive and have low GDP per capita
12. Trade barriers hurt development by protecting inefficient industries.
13. without direct access to the sea; landlocked nations do not have access to ocean trade routes and cannot easily trade their products with other countries.
14. *Market Economy*: economic decisions are made by the people and not the government; prices determined by supply and demand; people are free to own property and control their own labor. *Mixed Economy*: combine parts of both; both the market and the government are important; most countries have a mixed economy; the economy is market-oriented, but government has some role; United States has a mixed economy. *Command Economy*: people have little say as to how the economy should work; government owns the factors of production; government determines what is produced and all aspects of production.

Check for Understanding

1-2. individual freedom and high GDP per capita

3. The major difference is that in a market economy, individuals own the factors of production and make most economic decisions. In a command economy, the government makes the decisions and owns the factors of production.

4-5. Any two of the following: high population growth, trade barriers, landlocked, wars, large debt, corruption

The United States and Foreign Affairs, Lesson 1

What Do You Know?

Nations trade things they have for things that other nations have that they want.

trade wars, loss of international workers' jobs, disagreements of nations, conservation and pollution

Lesson Activities

Global Interdependence

1. Global Interdependence: is dependence of nations on each other to trade needed goods and services; this trade opens new markets, allows businesses to sell to other countries and make more money, and creates more jobs; Nations trade such things as food, oil, machinery, technology, and services.
2. Global interdependence is nations' reliance on one another for goods and services.
3. oil

Global Issues

4. Students should underline, "A trade barrier is any government policy that limits trade among nations."
5. A trade war is an economic conflict that occurs when nations put up trade barriers

to punish another nation for its trade barriers against them. They raise prices and reduce the choice of trade options for everyone.

6. educational system, skilled workers, industry, natural resources
7. Answers will vary.
8. Different resources, needs, and forms of government sometimes lead to different points of view.
9. flooding, mudslides, higher levels of carbon dioxide
10. Answers will vary; examples are using less gasoline to fight pollution, turning off lights when not in a room, turning off water when brushing your teeth, recycling materials
11. immigrants; refugees
12. *Who?* The global community is comprised of people and nations. *What?* Global interdependence exists and results in global trade. People and nations depend on one another for goods and services.

Check for Understanding

1. Nations need goods and services they cannot produce themselves. In order to get these items, they trade with other nations.

2-5. growing gap between rich and poor; political differences; environmental issues; immigration; tension between ethnic groups; refugees; terrorism; war; lack of food, clean water, health care

The United States and Foreign Affairs, Lesson 2

What Do You Know?

International organizations are a meeting of many people internationally to discuss important international issues and find solutions.

keep peace among nations, fight poverty, protect human rights, defend others who need defending, arrange trade agreements, fight disease

Lesson Activities

The Purpose of International Organizations

1. helping other nations in trouble, environmental problems, fights between countries, and trade and economic issues
2. Students should underline, "Diplomats are officials who represent their countries."
3. North Atlantic Treaty Organization, formed to defend its members
4. Governmental organizations are funded by their member nations. NGOs must raise the money needed to function on their own.
5. Possible answer: a success is the European Union's adoption of the euro; a failure is the persistence of terrorism despite great effort
6. poverty, education, economic development, health

International Organizations

7. The UN's main goal is to keep peace among nations. The General Assembly is where all nations meet, while the Security Council deals with world peace and security.
8. United Kingdom, China, France, Russia, U.S.
9. arrange trade agreements and settle trade disputes
10. the World Trade Organization and the Peace Corps; the first because global interdependence is based on trade, and the second because global interdependence will work more smoothly if the people of the world help each other
11. peacekeeping, medical care, economic development, environmental care, disaster response, education, poverty, and human rights
12. International Organizations are organizations that involve people from many nations. These organizations work to solve problems such as healthcare, education, and pollution. Examples would be: the UN (United Nations), NATO (North Atlantic Treaty Organization), WTO (World Trade Organization), WHO (World Health Organization), Peace Corps, and International Committee of the Red Cross.

Check for Understanding

1-3. deal with trade issues, find solutions to problems, help other countries

4. Student answers should demonstrate an understanding of the organization they chose.

The United States and Foreign Affairs, Lesson 3

What Do You Know?

Human rights are a protection or a freedom that all people should have.

Different types of government do not have the same level of freedoms as others, and this leads to conflict.

Lesson Activities

Human Rights

1. Human rights are protections or freedoms that all people should have.
2. It adopted the Universal Declaration of Human Rights, which defined the rights that all people should have.
3. freedom from arrest without cause, freedom from slavery, equal protection under law, the right to own property, the right to move about freely, the right to take part in government
4. China, Iran, Saudi Arabia, and North Korea
5. It protests governments that take away people's freedoms and sometimes refuses to trade with such countries.
6. They campaign around the world to end human rights abuses and bring attention of those abuses to the world.

Democracy, Liberty, and Conflict

7. communism and democracy
8. Students may say that in opposing communism, the United States helped advance human rights generally but in specific cases, acted to support rulers who abused human rights.
9. terrorism

Recent Conflicts

10. try to stop terrorist attacks on the U.S., reduce the threat of terrorist attacks, and help with recovery from attacks or other disasters
11. about seven years
12. Preventing terrorist attacks and terrorists from getting access to weapons of mass destruction have been the biggest foreign policy challenges for the United States since 2000.
13. Students should underline "President George W. Bush feared that terrorist groups might get **weapons of mass destruction (WMDs)."** and "Leaders believed that Iraq's dictator Saddam Hussein might give WMDs to terrorist groups."
14. terrorism
15. *Democracies*: usually protect human rights; about 60% of the world's nations are democracies; the United States has made the spread of democracy a foreign policy goal; *Non-democracies*: human rights are not always protected the same in non-democratic countries as they are in democratic countries; people are often treated poorly. Some countries discriminate against their citizens based on ethnicity, religion, sex, and other differences.

Check for Understanding

1. Without these basic rights, the quality of life is poor. In addition, human rights abuses can lead to crimes such as genocide.

2-3. clash of ideas of communism and democracy, United States tried to keep the Soviet Union from spreading communism, open warfare in Korea and Vietnam